The Growth of Love and Sex

JACK DOMINIAN, M.D.

WILLIAM B. EERDMANS PUBLISHING COMPANY
GRAND RAPIDS, MICHIGAN

© Jack Dominian and
National Children's Home 1982

First published in Great Britain in 1982 by Darton, Longman & Todd Ltd.
in association with the National Children's Home

This American edition published 1984 through special arrangement with Darton, Longman & Todd by William B. Eerdmans Publishing Company, 255
Jefferson Ave. S.E., Grand Rapids, Mich. 49503

Library of Congress Cataloging in Publication Data

Dominian, Jack, 1929-
The growth of love and sex.

1. Love (Theology)   2. Children — Sexual behavior.
3. Sex — Religious aspects — Christianity.   I. Title.
BV4639.D57   1984   241'. 66   84-1573
ISBN 0-8028-1988-5 (pbk.)

Contents

This book, which includes material from it, is published to coincide with the annual lecture to the Convocation of the National Children's Home given by Dr Jack Dominian in 1982 on The Growth of Love and Sex.

The National Children's Home Convocation Lectures have been published annually since 1946 and many are still available in book form. If you are interested, please write to the National Children's Home, 85 Highbury Park, London N5 1UD.

INTRODUCTION

Love and Sex in the Christian Tradition

Christians of all denominations have found considerable difficulty in reconciling their sexual experiences with the teaching they had received from their Churches. When such
teaching existed at all in the home it was often laden with a
sense of guilt which made men and women approach each
other later on in life with reticence and fear. Experiences
which should have been filled with joy and happiness became
excursions into furtive activity. The desirable appeared to
be forbidden. Even legitimate sexual activity within marriage
was surrounded by all sorts of taboos, prohibitions and
warnings.

It is not therefore surprising that in the sixties a wave of
sexual liberation swept through society which struck many
Christians as being a most welcome wind of change, whilst
for others it looked like a repudiation of all that was good
and familiar. Divorce began to soar, premarital sexual activity increased, sexual subjects were talked about freely in the
media and both adultery and fornication seemed to have
found their justification. The miniskirt became a symbol of
this new wave of rehabilitating the forbidden. In the midst
of these changes opposition grew in the form of people like
Mrs Whitehouse and Mr Muggeridge, and the feminist
movement asserted itself in denouncing the treatment of
women as mere sex objects.

Thus in the last twenty years a mixture of sexual attitudes
has arisen ranging from the most extreme permissive variety
to the remnants of the strict traditional ones. In the midst of
all this upheaval, Christians are reassessing the changes and
trying to make some sense of them. The process is not over
yet and this book is a contribution to the discussion.

A number of new factors need to be considered in this

1

debate. The first one is that traditional Christianity talked about love and sex as separate entities. The challenge of uniting the two remains an important but distant goal. One reason is that the intimate links between the two are not clearly understood. Psychology is very helpful here. As against the common view that the problems of sex and love begin at puberty, the studies of the last hundred years have shown that this is not so. As will be indicated in this book, the origins of both can be traced back into childhood.

If this is the case, then our training for sexuality and love needs to start from the very beginning of life. Some depth psychologists would claim that the interaction between baby and mother in the first few months is vital for the outcome of loving later on in life. Indeed there is a school of thought which considers that even intrauterine life is significant for the development of the personality in adulthood. These theories are much argued about. What is beyond dispute is that the foundations of love and sex are laid early in life, and if Christianity is to reassess its attitude to both topics it has to plumb the depths of the early years and understand the transactions between child and parents.

Another fundamental challenge is the reassessment of the meaning of sexual intercourse. In the past it was seen primarily as an act responsible for procreation. The development of the widespread availability of birth control has not only challenged this interpretation but has led to a fundamental revision of its meaning. This meaning is intimately linked with sexual pleasure. Sexual pleasure has been a stumbling-block to Christians since the very origins of their faith. A tradition surrounding it with suspicion and mistrust has come down to our very age. The separation between intercourse and procreation by birth control has accentuated the questions surrounding sexual pleasure. Is this pleasure to be freely available independently of any further meaning? Should it be available to all and sundry whether they are married or not? This particular question is central to Christian thought. Traditionally intercourse has been confined to marriage because children belong only to the latter institution. But as we have seen, birth control can effectively safeguard the act from its natural consequences. Why not just enjoy the pleasure and forget entirely its procreative possi-

2

bilities? This and similar questions face us currently and are awaiting urgent answers.

As our understanding of psychology deepens we are discovering that not all sexual behaviour can be simply understood on its objective basis. Thus not everyone who masturbates or has sexual intercourse behaves in this way with the same motivation and the same results. Men and women go through apparently the same experiences with vastly different consequences. There are people who get involved sexually but get very little sexual satisfaction. A married woman stated that when she was having sexual intercourse she was planning the menus for the following week. The springing up of vast numbers of sexual clinics in western society is an indication of how many people are either dissatisfied or fail completely to enjoy their sexual life. It suggests that physical functioning is not enough for sexual satisfaction, which is not surprising, when we remember that it is persons and not merely bodies that encounter each other.

The personal encounter is crucial to sexual satisfaction. If men and women reach each other with multiple wounds in their personalities received in the course of childhood, then their sexual experiences are bound to suffer from the consequences of their traumas. Thus men and women who feel unloveable as persons remain so even if they experience the heights of orgasmic satisfaction. Often however they do not experience even these peaks, because the wounds in them interfere with either normal sexual functioning or the receiving of sexual satisfaction. So the healing of these wounds in the growing person is a vital part of the task of enhancing sex and love.

We are living at a time of radical reassessment of the meaning of sexuality and we have the opportunity of a better understanding than ever before of the unity between love and sex. The specific questions we have to ask are how the experience of love grows from birth onwards and how this love can be fused with infant and adult sexuality. In answering these questions we will be exploring new areas of fundamental significance in Christian thought.

3

1

The First Year of Life

The newborn infant is entirely dependent for its survival on the care it receives from its parents, particularly mother. This care is primarily experienced through the body and so the quality of bodily contact is of fundamental importance to the baby. At this stage of its life the sense of good and bad is conveyed through physical sensations.

The first of these sensations is touch. In its intrauterine life it is bathed in a world of liquid which protects it from any rough contact. Although spontaneous movements of its limbs are part and parcel of its growth process, it is not yet receiving the sensation of touch from others. From the time of birth onwards human touch will become one of its principal sensations. Touch can be rough or smooth, gentle or fierce, light or heavy, warm or cold, painful and/or irritating. Gradually these sensations will become linked with the meaning of love.

With the passage of time the arms of the parents will become an invitation to pleasurable experiences. The extended arms of mother will gradually mean that the whole of the body will be enfolded gently and safely. The way the child is held is one of its first sensations of safety and therefore of *trust*. The body will now become a medium for security, an experience which will continue throughout life.

There are, however, babies who cannot rest quietly in the arms of their mothers for very long. They are restless and find it difficult to allow themselves to be held for any length of time. In the course of development they may overcome this restless phase and allow themselves to be held for longer periods. They may, however, persist in being able to tolerate only transient contact. These babies may grow into men and women who find physical touch difficult. Later on in life such people may not find it easy to convey good and pleasurable feelings with their bodies. This presents no problem if their partners do not need a lot of physical reassurance. But we do see at regular intervals couples who are ill-assorted over this point. One wants a lot of physical contact and the other finds it very difficult to give or share in such behaviour. The result can be a great deal of distress.

The fundamental point, however, is the realization that physical touch is at the centre of what we call love. From the very beginning of life outside the womb, touch begins to convey signals of proximity, safety, acceptance and feelings of being wanted. This physical contact becomes further differentiated with kisses, caresses and cuddling, and these particular actions progressively convey good feelings to the baby.

These good feelings have to be boldly contrasted with the opposite characteristics of being thrown, dropped, tossed across the room, banged or hit. These are the traumas to which the baby is subjected when it is battered. The battered baby learns the opposite sensations from love. It is subjected to pain and roughness, its limbs are broken and its body bruised. In these situations the body is the recipient of frustration, anger and even hate. Thus from a very early stage physical stimuli can range from pleasure to pain, and the body with its messages becomes a central channel for experiencing what is gradually going to become the meaning of love.

Physical touch is a very powerful sensation, but it is preceded and accompanied by vision and sound. The baby focusses on its mother's face when it is feeding, and her face becomes a site of great significance. In her face will be seen smiles or frowns, relaxation or tension, joy or tears, and the baby begins to associate these looks with a significant person in its life. Even more important at this stage—prior to speech—the baby will see in mother's face an invitation to understanding. It will gradually put together the feeling of being read accurately, and her face will mirror further the trust which comes from being loved and understood.

Of course, even without speech the baby can make its needs known by crying. Crying is a powerful way through which mother's attention is captured. But her attention is also spelled out when she addresses the baby by talking or singing to it.

Thus the baby is communicated with by touch, vision and sound, and these instinctual channels become the first means of registering loving feelings. These means of conveying loving feelings stay with us for the rest of our lives. At all significant moments of loving later on, touch, sound and vision become the means of conveying affection.

We fall in love with someone whose appearance attracts us visually, whose words and their contents we appreciate, and in whose arms we find care and attention. We make new friends in a similar way, and we maintain our relationships with gestures that invoke these three fundamental physical dimensions. In the world of intimate encounter all our adult means of getting to know others have been laid down in the first year of life when that which attracts and repels is learned in the arms of our mother.

These very obvious means of attachment were not always considered to be the crucial ones. An earlier conceptualization of attachment was that it was mediated through the mouth. The mouth is lined with a particular tissue called mucous membrane which offers pleasurable experiences when stimulated. Sucking the nipple was thought to be the first significant connection between mother and baby. We realize today that, important as this oral experience is, it is not the principal basis of attachment. But it has a historic importance in that it forms the first site of the body wherein Freud located infantile sexuality or libido. Libido or sexual drive came to be located in the mouth and its peak experience was held to be in the first year of life. The fact that the bonding between baby and mother is better understood in terms of the broader attachment of touch, vision and sound does not dismiss the importance of the mouth. The smooth lining on the lips, mouth and tongue remains a source of intense pleasure throughout life. The kiss has come to mean a loving gesture in many parts of the world, and the mouth can be a centre for erotic activity in adult life.

Reference has been made to the bonding process between mother and baby. In this process we witness one of the most awesome events of life. The baby has lived and been nurtured in the womb of mother for a period of nine months.

After birth this very same being is aided by nature to form a *relationship* with mother. This is the first relationship of love in each of our lives. It is the fundamental means through which we will learn to form an attachment of affection with another human being.

Within a matter of a short time the baby begins to recognize mother as she approaches the cot. The baby smiles, gradually lifts its arms to reach out to her, kicks in pleasure and satisfaction. It becomes alert to her sounds and will distinguish her presence from others. Thus, in the first few months of life a crucial bonding of affection and love is established and becomes the basis for the facilitation of the growth of the child. Such a bond is also effected with father and other people who are in constant contact with the baby.

This first bond in our life becomes the pattern for other attachments later on with friends, lovers and spouses. In particular we form with our spouse the second intimate relationship in our life. We are accustomed to a sort of closeness with our parents, particularly mother, in which touch, vision, sound and probably smell play such a crucial role that the same characteristics naturally play a similar role in our life of love as adults.

We hold our husbands and wives with the same tenderness and affection as that with which we were held in our first year of life. We watch our partners with the same intensity and scan their faces for signs of approval or disapproval. Not only do we examine their faces for the way they feel towards us, but we expect to be understood in depth without having to say a word, a similar understanding to that which we received as babies. The importance of communication between spouses has been highlighted in marriage counselling nowadays. It is, of course, perfectly true that we need to talk to our partners if they are going to receive and understand fully our inner world. But what most couples long for is that look of instant understanding which comes about without a word being said. It is a return to that state of innocent and instant contact between baby and mother in the first year of life when words were unnecessary for complete communication. Finally, when we do have to resort to words, these enrich the exchange; it is with words that we can conclude the miracle of love.

7

This sense of oneness which is achieved between baby and mother, expressed through touch, vision and sound, is of course repeated at frequent intervals in sexual intercourse. The body has now assumed a further meaning as the source of erotic excitation, and the union between the bodies is also genital, ultimately giving sexual pleasure. But the basic structure of affection is the fundamental one which we experienced very early in our lives. As lovers we hold each other's bodies, stroke, caress and kiss them. We look at each other with the same degree of tenderness as we first felt in the looks we exchanged with our mothers. We whisper softly words of seductive adoration which have the same stirring significance as at an earlier stage of our lives. Here then is the meeting-point of infantile and adult sexuality.

Another feature which transpires in this first year and is of great significance to love is the entry into our lives of the feeling of unconditional love. As babies we do not have to do anything to earn our mothers' approval. We are taken care of, we are loved because we exist. We don't have to please; we don't have to justify our worth; we are simply loved because we exist. This is the unconditional loving to which we try to return repeatedly in our intimate life later on. As we grow older we enter a different world of justification by work and deeds. Later in life we have to earn our approval, especially at work. We have to earn our money, compete for success, stand out in our achievements to receive praise. And yet we are longing for that instant but powerful welcome when we were received and mattered simply because we were there.

This experience of unconditional acceptance has profound implications both in our life of love and in that of our faith. God loves us unconditionally. Can we do anything to deserve God's love for us? The answer is no, we cannot make God love us more or less, because his love is infinite. Are we justified by faith or by good works? This question has been at the root of much theological debate; it opened a deep chasm in Christianity at the time of the Reformation, and we are trying to pick up the pieces today in the movement of unity amongst the Churches.

In fact justification by faith is the fundamental requirement. It is the requirement in which we open ourselves to

8

be loved. It is in fact our basic predisposition with which we enter the world. Our entry into this world is as loveable beings and our parents are our lovers. Being human they can and do make mistakes. God does not make mistakes. He loves us unconditionally so long as we let him. It is not a question of justifying ourselves by our actions, rather our actions have to ensure that we do not put obstacles to the unconditional loving of God.

But surely can we not please our parents and God by our specific actions? The real answer is that it is perfectly true we can and do please both by our specific actions; but we do not introduce a new dimension of loving in this way, we simply renew constantly the ever-present love of both. When it comes to our friends and spouses, we seek of course this unconditional love but in these relationships of friendship and marriage it is not so readily available, and our actions can be an inducement to further loving.

In the first year of life the sense of being loved is intimately linked with physical proximity. When we begin to separate from our mother physically a sensation of anxiety begins to creep in. This anxiety of separation is brought to an end by the appearance of mother. But what if she does not appear?

If we watch a baby lying in the cot just after waking up, it will look around for the familiar signs of mother. It may wait for a little while or even play. If it is able to pull itself up on the side of the cot, it will scan the room even more carefully. If mother is still missing, it will next use its lungs. It will cry. This will often bring the mother, who will pick up the baby, and the anxiety of separation will come to an end.

But what happens if mother is not forthcoming? What if she is in hospital or has left suddenly? It used to be thought that only mother could provide the baby with the attention it needed. We know now that any other familiar figure such as father or a nanny or granny can take the role of the mother. But what happens if there is no one? If, for example, the baby is in hospital and there is no one who is familiar to it? The answer is that the baby will go on crying for hours and sometimes for days; then it will stop and start playing. This used to be thought a sign that the baby had got over its separation anxiety. It is now realized that, far from getting

9

over its grief, the baby stops crying because it goes into a state of despair, despair which gradually moves into a state of detachment. It is no longer linked to its mother through affection, and if she returns some weeks later the baby may be uninterested in her. The attachment has to be formed afresh.

This is a pattern of grief reaction which all of us experience when we lose someone we love through the end of friendship, divorce or death. We go through the same anxiety of not being in touch with the missing person. We then grieve for the loss and cry as babies do. Finally we gradually learn to do without the person concerned but with a fundamental difference. If we have been in a relationship for a long time, we have internalized the physical image of our lost one and we can retain this image inside us. This is a process that occurs in the second year of life and we shall meet it in the next chapter.

Thus the first year of life is crucial for the experiences we call love. The fundamental fact is that we enter into relationship with our parents, particularly our mothers. We form a fundamental bond or attachment which becomes the prototype of all future intimate bonds of love. Within this bond we begin to experience love by being held and holding; by being seen and seeing the other as a significant figure; by being addressed and babbling back. The body is the crucial infrastructure of love. It is a love which we experience unconditionally. It is not a question of deserving it but rather of receiving it because we happen to exist. This is a love which we need not only for our survival but also for our development, and it depends on the continuing presence of a significant other: mother, father or usually both. Part of this physical love is situated in the mouth, which is both a site of affection and the first sexual orifice. The conjunction of affection and sexuality in the mouth is a forerunner of the intimate link that has to exist between the two throughout life.

2

The Second and Third Years of Life

During the second and third years the child begins to go through the first phase of independence or autonomy in the outline of development used by Erikson. This independence is the first step in the gradual separation between child and parents. During these two years the young child achieves an enormous amount. It learns how to crawl, stand up and ultimately walk. It acquires speech, learns to feed itself and gradually to dress itself.

Throughout all this period the child is going through an apprenticeship. It is learning how to look after itself, and the tutors are the parents, particularly the mother. A great deal depends on the way the mother facilitates this process. She needs understanding and—above all—patience. The child learns by trial and error. It will make mistakes. The food will be splashed all over its face and on the table and floor. Shoes will be put on the wrong feet and the buttons will take a long time to be managed efficiently. During all these experiments the young child's process can be facilitated by encouragement, praise and reassurance. On the other hand the child can be harassed, criticized and made to feel stupid for its untidy efforts. In other words it can be ridiculed, made to look foolish, embarrassed or ashamed. The way it is treated can make all the difference in the world to the way it feels about itself.

In the course of this phase of development the child can begin to feel pleased with its accomplishments. This pleasure takes the form of trust; trust in itself. If the opposite takes place, its sense of confidence begins to receive the first serious knocks. Instead of feelings of assurance, doubts begin to enter its inner world about its competence.

The sense of achievement in this period is intimately re-

11

lated to the experience of love of self. Christians raise their eyebrows at the mention of love of self, which has been associated with selfishness. In fact it is nothing of the sort. We are not constantly reminded in the Scriptures to love our neighbour as ourselves for no particular good reason. In order to be able to love our neighbour we need to have something good to offer, and basically the best we can give is ourselves. The second and third years of our lives are the period when the foundations of our self-esteem are established. This is a time when we can begin to feel that we possess ourselves and that what we own feels good. The sense of feeling loveable which begins to be felt in the first year continues in the second and third years when parents affirm our achievements and we begin to feel that we have greater command of our environment.

This experience of acquiring new skills does not cease with the second and third years of life. It goes on throughout childhood and affirmation is needed continuously. We need the encouragement of our friends and spouses to continue acquiring new skills in adult life.

As the child learns to walk it moves about the house and ventures outside. Progressively it can distance itself from mother and feel safe in her absence. Ultimately in the third year some children can attend a nursery school or playgroup and be away from mother for a few hours. This ability to be separated from mother and feel safe depends on the acquisition by the child of a picture of mother which it can retain in her physical absence. This is a process known as internalization. Mother remains alive and effective inside the child without being present. The ability to internalize significant figures in our lives is crucial for love and faith.

It is not possible for us to remain always in physical proximity to those we love. We have to be separated and ultimately we have to be separated definitely through death. One way that we can overcome the pangs of physical absence is to retain the image of the loved inside us in their absence. But what about God? We have to acquire a sense of God without ever seeing or touching him. The God we internalize is the one revealed to us in the Scriptures, rendered alive in the Church through symbols and other means and in the love we exchange between ourselves. We internalize our

12

distinct image of God depending on the influences in our lives, but we do so without seeing or touching him. The importance of this ability is shown in the Gospels when Thomas insists that he will not believe in Jesus' resurrection until he puts his finger in his wounds. Thomas was fortunate to receive this grace, but our Lord anticipated and blessed those whose faith would persist without the advantage of physical contact.

As the young child begins to explore its newly found world and acquire its autonomy, it is bound to enter into conflict with mother. Sooner or later it will go near places which are forbidden, touch and possibly break important objects, and try to have its way, opposing that of mother. Such conflict is inevitable. The irritated—at times frustrated—mother may shout, smack and, at the extreme end of the scale, damage the child, although the latter is rare.

In the course of conflict, the child will begin to feel bad, sad and guilty when it realizes that it has displeased mother. Normally these feelings are transient and restoration of good feelings is rapid. But here the child meets, perhaps for the first time, the whole cycle of badness, guilt, reparation and forgiveness. The child will learn that mother can become cross, displeased and upset. When she is like this her child will feel cut off from her love temporarily and, at the same time, the sense of badness and guilt enters its life. It also learns rapidly that restoration of good relationships can be achieved with what will gradually become a sequence of regret and sorrow, reparation and the ultimate forgiveness.

This cycle of conflict, offence, hurt, damage, guilt and the sense of badness, followed by distress, sorrow, reparation and forgiveness remains with us throughout life. It is an essential ingredient of the meaning of love. We learn early in our lives that we can hurt those we love, and this knowledge causes a peculiar anxiety which we experience as the pain of guilt, which remains with us until such time as we are forgiven. There are men and women with long memories who remember parents who were extremely difficult to appease; parents who took a long time to forgive and who withdrew into a sullen and hurt state for long periods, making them feel terrible at what they had done and caused their actions to assume the quality of a heinous crime; other par-

13

ents who would not accept apologies but insisted on making them feel particularly bad and humiliated whenever they did anything wrong. Such experiences of humiliation and guilt may make us feel deeply reluctant to apologize when we become adults because we cannot contemplate ever being in the wrong, such is the severity of pain associated with wrongdoing. In these circumstances our parents did not treat us as if the matter was transient, easily understood and forgiven but made us feel wicked.

Grown-ups remember from childhood devastating experiences of being punished or—worse—ignored when they had committed some wrong and finding it difficult or impossible to return rapidly and easily into a restored state of love. This acute sense of wickedness may have been extended into the way the child felt in relation to God. The unmoved, angry or withdrawn parent is now linked with God, who is also pictured as an irreparably hurt divinity. Ultimately some children grew up feeling that it was their badness which crucified their parents and Christ.

These illustrations are in fact in contrast with how the majority of parents deal with misdemeanours, which are quickly forgiven and forgotten even if some punishment intervenes. Punishment is accepted at this stage and in the immediate years to come as something justified which rectifies the wrongdoing. Wrongdoing and punishment in these early years are concrete. The sophisticated nuances of motive and intention will enter later in the life of the child. Now justice is rough and summary with few modifications. If a vase is broken its worth does not matter; it is a vase and that is that. Punishment has to meet the crime and few allowances are made. But the ordinary child expects to be forgiven, and gradually it learns that the forgiveness which restores a loving relationship is also attained with God.

God, like our parents, is ready to forgive with the minimum of fuss if we, in turn, are saddened by and sorry for the distress we have caused. Perhaps no role of parents is as important as their ability to restore the state of love in their relationships with their children, just as God does all the time. The truly loving parent will gradually help the child understand that their loving relationship is never broken but merely interrupted when the relationship is damaged. In the same way our relationship with God is never destroyed except on those rare occasions when we deliberately and clearly wish to cease having a relationship with him at all.

Conflict, guilt, punishment bring about in these second and third years of life the awareness of *ambivalence*, that is to say that we can love and be angry with the same person. The young child, who in the first year has learned to expect nothing but approval from mother, is suddenly astonished when she shouts, admonishes or even smacks. The same source can now issue different messages, one moment those of love, the next those of anger and pain. The toddler has to begin to cope with these conflicting experiences. At this stage in its life it cannot cope with any degree of anger from mother; it needs her too much and so it will learn to avoid upsetting her. But this will gradually bring tension in its life. The pursuit of independence is often accompanied by the need for rebellion and disobedience. It requires a near enough perfect matching of parents and children to ensure that parents permit just what is appropriate for the next phase of the child's growth. The gap between what the child desires and what the parents think is appropriate provides always some ground for conflict which appears to be inevitable.

In the course of this conflict and ambivalence the scene is set for the fluctuating state of love between two people. In the end a loving relationship depends on the fact that we love the significant people in our life more than we are angry with them, indifferent to them or even hate them. In our major relationships we have to ensure that our positive feelings are greater than our negative ones, and that balance depends greatly on whether our parents made it relatively easy and possible in our childhood to restore a positive state in our relationship whenever it was threatened with overwhelming negative feelings. Since we are all subject to anger from our earliest years, our parents have to give us room to ventilate our anger without making us feel guilty in doing so. The importance of registering and expressing our anger without fear is a vital part of our education as children. So many people reach adult life unable to recognize their anger or, if they do so, feeling compelled to hold it back or, when they express it, being overwhelmed by a powerful sense of

15

guilt. The ability to feel angry and still retain one's sense of goodness and value is a vital part of mature growth, facilitated by our parents.

One of the principal areas where conflict may occur is over toilet-training. In these second and third years, the mother is keen to get her child to void its faeces in the appropriate receptacles and not in the nappies. Most children learn how to do so with encouragement and praise. For some children, however, toilet-training can become a battleground. The mother wants one thing and the child will not oblige. It realizes for the first time that it can control its own destiny in this matter. It can pass a motion or withhold it. It can give or retain. It can yield or stubbornly resist.

For Freud the anus becomes the second orifice of importance. In the first year the mouth gave rise to the oral phase; now in these years the anus gives rise to the anal. Like the mouth, the anus is lined with a sensitive mucous membrane which gives rise to pleasurable sensations when touched. Thus for Freud the anus becomes another erotogenic zone and another site where libido is situated. The connection between pleasurable sexual sensations and defaecation makes faeces and the nomenclature surrounding the subject an extremely fertile area for scatological jokes.

The anus becomes another orifice which from childhood onwards combines pleasurable and excretory sensations and in adult life assumes genital sexual connotations. Many people, including Christians, want to draw a veil over this area and these activities, particularly the sexual ones. As a result much that appertains to them is siphoned off into pornography and fringe literature.

This will not do. The young child has no notion of dirt. Its bowel action is a normal pleasurable activity, provided the parents treat it as such. If they do, the sensations associated with that part of the anatomy will not be treated as a guilty secret but will become part of the child's world of loving exchange with those whom it trusts.

Thus these years move the child into a crucial exchange of love between itself and its parents. The long process of separation has begun. Physical and emotional separation are inevitably surrounded by conflict and ambivalence, and the child has to learn from now on to cope with mixed feelings

16

for the same loved person. On balance it must learn to love more than to be angry or hateful, and this it achieves as its parents affirm its goodness and reduce the badness of its guilt. In the process of this exchange of love, another part of its anatomy—the anus—is brought into focus, and the fusion between love and sexuality continues and takes the child to the next stage of its development.

3

The Fourth and Fifth Years of Life

The fourth and fifth years of life are important for they form the last remnants of total home life. The child becomes a small adult in its own home.

It can roam around in the house and the surroundings and it acquires a sense of initiative in this phase of its life. There is a feeling that it can control the world around it. It can walk, run, climb, talk fluently and, if a bit advanced, read. It knows where it stands with its parents and its only competitors are older or younger brothers and sisters. Their advent can cause jealousy but, if the parents are careful, this feeling need not deepen and it can be a passing phase.

One way by which jealousy can be avoided is to ensure that each child receives a proper allocation of time, care and affection as is appropriate to its needs. At this point, having mentioned jealousy, it is worth making the simple distinction between envy and jealousy. Envy is the prior experience and belongs to a twosome relationship. It is a feeling of being disturbed by the qualities or things possessed by another which the envious person wishes belonged to him. In simple terms we want to have what another person has. Envy arises in the first few years of life when we have intense and exclusive relationships. We are small, limited, weak; our parents appear big, with endless resources, powerful and strong, and we would like to be like them. Envy, however, is more than a desire to imitate. It is a wish to remove from the person what he or she has and to make it our own. We resent the fact that they have what we do not. Envy, like all the other characteristics—positive and negative—acquired in the early years, can remain with us throughout life and at its ultimate point lead us to damage and destroy the person we envy.

Jealousy on the other hand is a threesome matter. At its root is the fear of losing someone or something we have and appreciate to somebody else. Freud referred to the triangular situation between child and parents and in outlining his famous Oedipus complex drew some startling conclusions. According to him the little boy is sexually attracted to mother. Sexually in this context means that he wants her attention and care, which are, of course primarily physical, but *note not* genital at this stage. This desire makes father a competitor and therefore someone to try to exclude from mother. But father cannot be excluded. Indeed the boy fears father in fantasy and the fear is the loss of the penis through castration. So ultimately the boy gives up his fantasy intentions regarding mother and sides with his father, whose manhood now becomes the pattern with which the young boy identifies; in this way the Oedipus complex is resolved. All this may sound a wild speculation on the part of Freud. But we certainly see the phenomenon of what we call 'mother's boy', in which a boy fails to disengage from the proximity of mother during the growing years, resulting sometimes in sexual variations such as homosexuality or cross-dressing. The opposite is said to occur with the little girl who harbours sexual wishes for father which have to be given up before the girl identifies with her mother. This pattern of behaviour is known as the Electra complex.

The classical triangular situations between siblings and parents are far more readily understood. Sometimes these jealousies are encouraged by the attitude of parents. Some parents favour a boy at the expense of a girl or the more intelligent child at the expense of the less gifted, or give more attention to the child who is handicapped or ill. The way to avoid jealous reactions is to make each child feel unique and that its needs are treated and met as such.

The needs for affection continue in these years, but as children grow the occasions for sitting on their parents' laps, being hugged and cuddled become less. How does the child continue to receive love and affection at a distance during these years? This is a matter which does not receive much attention in text-books. The way affection is communicated increasingly as the child grows is through feelings of being recognized, wanted and appreciated.

As far as recognition is concerned, the child is no longer picked up and hugged as it was in the previous years. It is recognized by being greeted with joy. Its arrivals and departures are noted and appropriately surrounded with enthusiasm. Later on in life some men and women will complain that the significant persons in their lives will not recognize them. Spouses will complain of partners who come downstairs in the morning without greeting them, sit behind a newspaper at breakfast and say nothing. They will leave home with a perfunctory goodbye and on return resume this total failure to recognize, greet or speak to their partners. These may be shy, introverted people of both sexes or wounded adults who during their childhood felt ignored or were ignored. The word 'felt' is used because in fact some of these people did not lack attention but for some individual reason in their make-up could not register this recognition.

Recognition is developed into the feeling of being wanted. The child continuously notes the feelings of its parents when it is in their presence. The alacrity with which its needs are met, the frequency with which it is played with and the way its spontaneous contributions are received all gradually add up to a feeling of being wanted. The child registers all the time whether its presence is an occasion for rejoicing or a cumbersome responsibility. The child learns when it is treated as a nuisance and when it is appreciated as a person. Later on in life adults will also rapidly rate when they feel wanted or ignored; when they are used or exploited instead of being wanted for their own sakes.

Finally, beyond recognition and feeling wanted, the sense of love is added when the child feels appreciated; that is to say when its talents, worth and abilities are not only recognized but responded to with relish. Earlier I remarked that the first experience of love is unconditional acceptance from the very fact that we exist. As we grow up our existence expresses itself in various positive and negative ways. The ways these behaviour characteristics are received makes a lot of difference to the way we grow in love. If the positive features are acknowledged and rejoiced in and the negative ones ignored or suitably punished, then we continue to grow in an affirmative style. If our positive features are ignored and the negative ones specially selected for criticism, re-

20

monstration and punishment, then we emerge as adults aware only of our faults and limitations. This is of special importance later on in life in the way we treat others, particularly our intimate friends and spouses. Some people, however, have a peculiar habit of only noticing in their friends and spouses that which is wrong and ignoring everything that is positive, which passes unnoticed and unappreciated. We tell them and convince ourselves that we help them best by pointing out their limitations. In fact we do not do anything of the sort either as parents or as adults. If we notice only the things that are wrong, then those concerned will only respond to messages of correction, finally feeling worthy of notice only when they are reprimanded. Most parents and spouses both criticize and praise, and in the triad of recognition, wanting and appreciation love continues to flow through the spoken word.

Since this is a book about love which helps the growing person to feel loveable, we have also to consider parental behaviour which instead of affirming and loving leads to insecurity, doubt and fear. Bowlby sums up five ways in which these psychological handicaps can occur, and the years which we are considering are those when children begin to become aware of these traumatic relationships.

The first, already mentioned, is one in which either parent persistently ignores the needs of the child for love or actively disparages it or rejects it. There are parents who not only do not love their children physically, who do not recognize, want or appreciate them, but actually tell then what a nuisance they are, punish them severely and disproportionately and make it absolutely clear how much happier they would be without their children. This is the pattern of overt rejection.

The second is discontinuation of parenting. I have shown how limited the capacity of children is in their early years to retain the sense of being loved. If they are moved from person to person, institution to institution, place to place in these early years and even later on, children experience no continuity of care and loving. No sooner has a child established a sense of continuity, reliability and predictability than it is moved and it has to start from scratch all over again. If this upheaval happens frequently, then the child will give up the attempt to establish relations of affection afresh. These are the children who withdraw into themselves and build a world around them which shields them from further making and breaking of affectionate bonds. Their capacity to make these bonds has been blunted and for them people lose their significance of love. They simply become objects of servicing, good or bad servicing, but with no deeper experience of love allowed.

The same limitations once applied to long periods of hospitalization with infrequent visits from parents. Thus children, for example with orthopaedic illness, had to stay for long periods away from significant persons. Their companions were other children and nurses who changed frequently. Apart from reacting to the embarrassing experiences of hospital life, sick children also withdraw into themselves because the world of continuity, reliability and predictability has disappeared. Increasingly, as we are aware of the need of preserving bonds of affection, the isolated world of the hospital has been replaced by the frequent presence of parents, by nurses who do not change over rapidly and by a much closer look at the emotional needs of such children.

The third way is the use of love as a bargaining weapon by parents. The child needs parental love for its security as it needs nourishment for its physical survival. As I have tried to show, love means physical appreciation, meeting of needs, affirmative acknowledgement, wanting and appreciation on the positive side and the absence of neglect and cruelty on the negative side. Some children are tortured by their parents, particularly the mother, who uses the withdrawal of love or the threat of it as a means of disciplining the child. Such a child lives in a world of terror that its tenuous links with mother will snap at the next act of misdemeanour. In fact some parents do withdraw love for long periods as a form of punishment by not talking to their children, ignoring their presence, failing to show affection. As the child grows it begins to rely much less on this parental love for its survival. It has to learn to cope with these threats and it gradually becomes immune to them. But in doing so it also loses the ability to trust anybody as a source of love. It will rely instead on transient satisfaction, such as drink, drugs or sex,

22

and in the process use and exploit people. Sometimes the child is not strong enough to withdraw and remains pathetically dependent on the whims of its parents who blow hot and cold and are constantly threatening to withdraw their love. In these circumstances the child may be overcome with fear and toe the line. All its normal and healthy independence disappears and may reveal itself many years later on in marriage when it is inappropriate.

The fourth way is the threat not of withdrawing love but of leaving the family. This can coerce a child or a spouse but it can implant profound fears in children who are living with the constant dread of being abandoned. Many years later people who have lived through such a childhood will remember these threats and recoil with horror. Such is their fear that they suppress their own anger and avoid confrontation in their own marriages. They will remember long nights of lying awake in bed with their parents quarrelling and threatening to leave. They remember the agony of going to school and waiting with anxiety for home time in order to be reassured that their parents were still there.

The departure does not have to be physical. The threat can be a matter of life and death. There are parents who try to control their children by threatening that their disobedience will make them ill and kill them. Such threats can continue right up to adult life, and it takes a great deal of courage to stand up to such emotional blackmail. Sometimes the arguments are entirely between the spouses who threaten to leave each other. If the child is not old enough to understand what is going on, it may think that it is personally contributing to the tension and that it is its own fault that the parents are quarrelling or threatening to leave.

The fifth way is an escalation of the last one. Now the parent threatens to leave, to kill the other or even to commit suicide. The last two are not uncommon; unfortunately a great deal of parasuicide (suicidal attempts), suicide itself and murder are caused by family distress. The child here is caught in a situation which it hardly knows how to handle. Surrounded by threats of death, concerned whether its own behaviour is contributing to the drama and terrified of losing its main source of security, it lives a life of acute insecurity, never knowing when the blow will fall. If one of the parents

23

attempts suicide, its worst fears are reinforced and it lives with the dread that one day it will wake up and be an orphan.

All these ways can keep a child at the other end of the continuum of love. Instead of love it lives a life of fear, insecurity and the dread of abandonment. It can protect itself by surrounding itself with a shield of indifference or live in a precarious state of constant anxiety. In either case its ability to form secure attachments later on is imperilled unless there are some secure adults such as aunts, uncles, grannies, grandfathers or suitable substitutes with whom it can take refuge.

Needless to say that sexuality within such insecure relationships will also suffer. But in the absence of such a disturbing situation Freud sees in these years the culmination of the libidinal development of infancy. The third and final erotogenic zone is the genital one. The little boy will identify with his penis and the little girl with her vagina. These are the years when children begin to play at doctors and nurses, when they will investigate each other's bodies, when they will notice their genitals and even play with them. These are the years when questions about the origin of babies will commence.

Parents have the task of remaining unshocked in these situations. They have to begin to find the right language to describe the body and the appropriate imagination to talk about intercourse and fertilization. Provided the truth is preserved, the language and the description need only fit the needs of individual children. The language will vary from terminology which is familiar to the family to more technical and medical terms. The same questions will return year after year and the answers have gradually to become more sophisticated, but the truth has always to be preserved.

Thus these years which see the beginning of development of children into small adults will consolidate their sense of being loveable, something which is achieved by a mixture of physical and emotional exchanges in close and distant encounters. These are also the years when traumas of abandonment begin to seize the inner world of the child in insecure homes. Finally this is also the phase when infantile sexuality reaches its developmental conclusion.

4

The School Years

The years covered by the entry into the primary school are important in that they introduce the child into another world. So far its experience has been in the intimate world of its family, a world characterized by close personal relationships between itself and its parents, brothers and sisters and relatives. It is not a world which normally makes strenuous demands for care and attention. The child learns the feelings of love in the community of love called the family and is gradually accustomed to be treated as a person of worth and value.

The entry into the school brings the child into a world characterized primarily by impersonal relationships. It is now entering the community of life in which personal love takes second place and impersonal encounters are the order of the day. This is not to say that the pupils lack personal attention in most primary schools. They do not; but there are twenty to thirty in a classroom, and the individual attention of home has to be replaced by a community concern in which the children share the attention of the teacher.

The child enters the world of industry and competition, and from now on it has to work hard for appreciation. Approval is not automatic and unconditional as it has been at home. The young person begins to realize that there are others who can read, write, draw and do lessons better and who get praise for it. The adult world of earning one's way in life begins to enter that of the child. There is still a long way to go before one has to stand entirely on one's own feet, but the primary school is the beginning of a reality that is not based on personal love, although primary school teachers still maintain a good deal of the home atmosphere.

It is also a world that is governed by impersonal rules.

The school is a community which has to be regulated by what is right and proper for everyone. The individual style of love at home between parent and child has to give way to an impersonal world with rules and regulations that apply equally to everybody. Justice is of course tempered by a good deal of understanding of the limitations of primary-school children. Nevertheless the child gradually realizes for the first time that, if the school is to run smoothly, then it has to have rules and regulations which have to be obeyed for the good of the whole community. A realization of the *social* aspects of life begin to dawn. The whole of education is a preparation for the social aspects of life, and from now on the child will distinguish the two worlds of home and school with their different atmosphere and expectations.

During the second half of the primary-school years the young boy or girl will experience a further stage of autonomy. The sense of absolute rightness of those in authority will be challenged, and the worlds of both home and school will reverberate with cries of 'It is not fair'. The child's idea of justice begins to alter. Misdemeanours and breaking of the rules are no longer treated on a simple 'eye for an eye' principle. The older primary school child begins to realize a good deal more about motives and intentions, and crimes are not judged merely by their size. Justice and punishment have now to fit the misdemeanour in all its subtle details, and allowances have to be made for the inner world of the child.

Love is now understood in terms of what is appropriate in a community made up of adults and children who are related to each other not by intimate bonds of affection but by mutual concern. Friendships are struck up and new loyalties are established which have to be maintained constantly on the basis of renewed interest and mutual consideration.

In this school community there is a chance to undo some of the damage at home. Children who find themselves ignored at home can receive personal attention from the staff. Those rejected at home can begin to experience acceptance at school from the teachers. Individual teachers can in fact give special attention to particularly deprived children, and in the course of their work they can offer to children lacking

26

confidence in themselves a special affirmation to raise their sense of worth.

At the sexual level the child is not going through any spectacular sexual changes. Some boys and girls may see the beginning of puberty at the end of the primary school years, but this is a rarity. Some children, however, recall a marked genital awareness and remember masturbatory sexual activity without an emission. The correct approach for an adult is to understand the behaviour of the child before reaching conclusions. The youngster may be a solitary, withdrawn child who finds comfort in such an experience without understanding its full meaning. There may be mutual masturbation activity, or the youngster may be introduced to this behaviour by an older boy or even by an adult.

Finally there may well be occasions when the child experiences incest at home. Incest is not as rare as is imagined and girls in the primary school may be involved. When such an instance is discovered the whole family needs help, and above all the child involved must be handled in a way that does not detract from its future appreciation of genital activity. That is, the goodness of sex must be preserved and the particular inappropriateness defined. Under no circumstances must the child be threatened or frightened in incest cases, and every care should be taken to maintain or restore its relationship with the involved parent, who is often the father.

During these years children will return to the themes of intercourse, fertilization, pregnancy and young babies. As already indicated, the children will ask progressively more sophisticated questions and the parents and teachers have to instruct with accuracy and authenticity. Biological teaching at school in particular has not only to instruct in the physiology of new life but to emphasize constantly that new life has to take place within a setting of love which we call marriage.

The primary school years are a time when the child is introduced to a social community where there is personal concern but which is also an impersonal world run by rules and regulations. Within this community the worth of the child is attained by its personality but even more important by its scholastic achievements. Thus there is realization of

27

worth and merit by competence, effort, perseverance and the willingness to adapt to new modes of acceptance. During these same years the child is advancing towards puberty. Some children will anticipate this phase by genital activity and a few others will be aroused sexually by adults. Whatever the circumstances the goodness of sexuality has to be preserved and the trauma of the unwarranted invasion diminished.

5

Healing in the First Decade

The concept of healing has already been introduced in the primary school. There is a further important role of healing for those who take the place of parents when the latter cannot cope. Before I discuss their contribution I would like to say something in general about healing.

The concept of emotional healing is not a particularly scientific one although all human beings have some sense of it in their lives. It plays a more important part in the life of faith, when God is conceptualized as someone who heals. For most people the matter rests there. Healing arises in the hands of God and how it is achieved is not something which receives much attention. But healing through the power of God, mediated via prayer, is ultimately the result of a relationship. People who put their trust in God open themselves to respond to the call of God which brings about the desired change. No healing can take place if human beings are closed to God's effective intervention.

The person who heals is someone important in our lives. His or her contribution is the same as that of a parental figure. The modern introduction to this concept of healing comes through psychoanalysis. Freud was the first person who was prepared to listen to what a patient had to say unreservedly. In the course of listening at regular intervals, the patient began to experience Freud as a parental figure and to relive some important events of childhood with him. By reliving these events the patient had a second chance to negotiate afresh what went wrong the first time round with the real parent. In this way healing takes place. The therapist becomes temporarily a significant person in the life of the patient and has the opportunity to sort out distortions of feelings. In real life healing also takes place by significant persons who give us new loving experiences of stability, trust and affirmation and replace unreliability, mistrust and rejection. The trouble of course is that healing is not brought about by a straightforward replacement of some experience by another. The child who is emotionally wounded reacts to hurt by protecting itself from the damaging situation. Those who encounter it later on have first to penetrate the shields of defence before they can make an impact and this requires tack and patience.

Let us now look at some of the patterns of defence with which the child protects itself in this first decade. There are essentially three such patterns. The first one is withdrawal. The hurt child gradually refuses to open itself to emotional interaction. It will not enter into an exchange of feelings but remains deliberately cut off from others so that they have no longer the power to please or displease. This is a more refined attitude than that taken in the world of animals, who under threat can either fight back or fly. A withdrawal is a subtle form of flight in which the child is afraid of being hurt again, so it keeps its distance from adults and simply lives a life of its own.

The second is a belligerent attitude. In this response the child is prepared to fight everyone to avoid being hurt again. Every approach is met by aggression and non-co-operation. The only thing the child knows is to protect itself against further intrusion in its life and that defiance is the best form of protection. Such a child needs understanding, for behind its aggression lies a desire for closeness and affection.

The third approach, which is very close to the second, is continuous testing. The child will allow itself to be approached by those who have taken over its life, but it will be suspicious of their intentions. At regular intervals it will provoke a fight, it will disobey some elementary rule and in this way it will test the intentions of those who claim to love it. Such a testing approach must not be confused with the normal process of challenging authority which is a progressive seeking of independence. The child who is testing the authenticity of its caretakers will do so more often and more awkwardly and will be difficult for the sheer devilment of it.

Now we can take a look at the way healing can take place in the presence of these three reactions. If the child is withdrawn, how will it react to the efforts made to overcome a sense of rejection? discontinuity of caring? love as a bargaining weapon? or the sense of abandonment?

At the heart of healing the withdrawn youngster is the need to build a relationship afresh. From those surrounding the child someone will emerge who has a special place in the child's reactions. Such a man or woman needs to direct attention to establishing a new relationship with the child. This task can be approached with both words and actions. Initially the child will remain aloof or be involved for short periods and then withdraw again. Every time it makes a move towards the selected person, such an approach should be rewarded with obvious joy and pleasure. The timetable of returning to a relationship may be long—a matter of months—or short—a matter of weeks. But whatever the time taken, the person concerned must be patient and in particular not show disappointment when the child withdraws. An adult needs support during such a testing time.

When rapport has been established, there is a need for affirmative acceptance; that is to say the child needs to feel safe from the apprehension that anything which goes wrong will be met by rejecting disapproval. In this situation those in charge have a problem with discipline. What happens when such a youngster breaks the rules? A wounded child needs to be assured that its pronounced hurt will not be reopened. Admonition must be carried out with care and love so that the child does not feel betrayed again. Another form of betrayal which the child will be looking for is the loss of the person with whom new ties have been established, and therefore continuity of care is paramount. Such continuity of care is to be found not only in the presence of the person concerned, but in the day-to-day fulfilment of promises made. Children need not only continuity but reliability and predictability, and the hurt person is particularly vulnerable in these areas. For them a let-down is magnified and the sense of abandonment or fear of losing their newly loved person is never far away. If the person with whom a new relationship has been established has to be absent through illness, time off or holiday, then the child needs to understand the circumstances by having them spelled out clearly. Finally, it goes without saying that such a youngster should

31

not have its newly discovered love and trust treated as a bargaining weapon. Whatever the hurts an adult is subjected to in the process of forming a relationship afresh, the tenuous new attachment must never be strained by emotional blackmail. Furthermore such a caretaker must remember that a child has a rich fantasy world and must be careful to listen to it so that any misconceptions the child may feel about hurting its new friend are understood and corrected.

The belligerent child who is constantly angry and sullen is no easier to handle. Such a child feels rejected all the time and has learned to behave in a way that means rejection will be continued. Someone befriending such a child must first accept that it has a very much limited capacity for frustration. Rejection is never far off from the mind of such a child. It expects to be torn off a strip, possibly hit or punished. The first task of the caretaker is not to react in this way, but to receive the child's onslaught and not to retaliate. Some children express their aggression physically and destructively. These children can be restrained initially and at a later stage encouraged to let off steam by some aggressive activity— playing soccer, learning to box or even just hitting a cushion—in this way alleviating the excess of energy which they need to discharge.

As in the previous pattern, continuity of care is vital. The child is sometimes filled with fantasies that its aggression has damaged or destroyed those who are attempting to love it. If these people go away or disappear, its worst fears may be confirmed. Another fantasy is that it has been abandoned as a punishment for its aggression. The worker concerned must be able to show that he/she is not easily damaged or destroyed. This does not mean that aggression has to be encouraged. The child needs gradually to learn that it can receive care and attention without having to resort to aggression. Its non-aggressive efforts have to be praised and appreciated.

As with the withdrawn child—but particularly so with the aggressive one—there will come the time when discipline has to be enforced. Discipline has to be distinguished from *retaliation*. So far in its life such a child has expected to be hit back with words or physically. It now has to learn that aggression is not the way to be treated. Gradually it can be shown that life needs order and that aggression can destroy the routine of life. Punishment can be the withdrawal of privileges, but it must be seen to be fair and without a sense of retaliation. Such a child will gradually come to realize that it is being treated as someone who matters and not simply as an aggressive object. All this takes time and of course, as soon as some new relationship is established and appears firm, the child will do something to test the validity of the situation. Adults have to realize that they are being tested; and when they fail, because they are fallible, they must be prepared to start afresh. In order to do this those taking care of deprived children have to have support to cope with such disappointments.

Often children do not resort to these patterns of defence. Rather they are keen to receive as much approval and love as possible so they are eager to please and co-operate. They appear to be happy and contented and most of them are so. But some of these children who keep their anger, disappointment and frustration under control may at some time let go and all hell is temporarily let loose.

All these various patterns require elaboration. For the sake of clarity they have been distinguished in this chapter; often, however, they are present as a mixture of features. The point to remember is that most children, except those who are very seriously hurt, are ready and eager to form a second and third relationship in life. The need for affection and love remains strong. Despair and cynicism are still rare in this first decade and so the possibility of healing remains.

Some of these children will of course return to their homes and to their parents. The need to continue the relationships which have been formed in the interval remains. Those who provide a second and third relationship remain important in the life of the child and continous contact is one way of ensuring that the child does not feel betrayed yet again.

6

The Challenge of Puberty and Adolescence

The advent of puberty is characterized by the emergence of the secondary sexual characteristics in both sexes. For the girl this means monthly menstruation, development of breasts and the growth of pubic hair. For the boy puberty means the growth of the male distribution of hair in the face, chest and pubes, the change in the voice and the enlargement of the penis. All these physical characteristics which occur for girls around the age of twelve to thirteen and for boys between thirteen and fourteen are the product of complex physiological and hormonal changes in the body.

Psychologically the emphasis begins to shift from affective relationships to sexual ones. Boys and girls begin to look at each other with a new awareness which is focussed on their physical appearance. Inwardly these developments may be welcomed if they have been properly anticipated, or approached with fear if the body is invaded with changes which are not properly understood.

Both sexes become very conscious of themselves and dress both to hide and to accentuate the newly discovered physical characteristics. Both menstruation for the girl and spontaneous emission on the part of the boy are sudden events and may take both sexes by surprise. Time is needed to come to terms with these changes and their meaning. At first both sexes feel awkward and uncomfortable with their bodily transformations. Boys watch their faces anxiously to decide when a beard is sufficiently present to merit shaving. Girls become conscious of the size of their breasts and gradually aware of menstrual pain or discomfort or even premenstrual tension with fluctuations of mood. At this stage in the proceedings the meaning of puberty, however well explained, hardly registers. The facts that every month brings ovulation

34

in the girl and that the semen is loaded with millions of sperms are not things young adolescents concentrate on.

Rather they are concerned with appearance and how they hit it off with those of the opposite sex. The accent is on the body and its sexual experiences. Almost invariably boys—and frequently girls—will experiment in the solitary isolation of their beds and discover that their genitals contribute to pleasurable experiences. These pleasurable experiences will gradually be related to sexual attraction. Over months and years young adolescents will become conscious of their bodies as both a source of attraction and a source of pleasure.

For a while these two experiences will dominate their lives. The ability to attract people of the opposite sex will be regarded as important, but at the same time they will congregate with groups of their own sex and their peers will be their principal mentors. They will compare their sexual appearance and prowess amongst themselves. Boys will compare the size of their penises and girls will be aware of the size of their breasts.

At the same time that this process of bodily change is occurring, some adolescents go through a psychological crisis. They may become so intensely aware of their appearance that they become over-sensitive about it. There are girls and boys who become so anxious about their appearance that they will not go out at all. One such girl, who became markedly anxious about her appearance, used to come back from work, undress, put on her dressing-gown and refuse to leave her room. Young men with acne may gradually become extremely anxious about their appearance and afraid to go to dances or mix with others. In all these situations we may be watching an exacerbation of previous anxieties about meeting others or the onset of new ones which appear now for the first time.

Whether the advent of puberty is normal or in some way abnormal, the body becomes the principal means of communication. In a way this is a reminder of the child's first year, when the body was so important in communicating. This time, however, looks, touch and sound are primarily fused with erotic messages. Both sexes are communicating through their bodies, which are charged with sexual meaning. Friendships characterized by acknowledgement, support, acceptance, co-operation and joint activity do not cease to exist; but year by year the erotic element stands out and introduces yet another dimension, namely the relationship with the parent.

The erotic body now intervenes between parents and children and the incest taboo is firmly established. Parents can and do show affection to their children, but care is taken not to express this affection in any sexual sense. Children present themselves as sexual objects to their parents but the latter must not engage in any sexual activity, however innocent it may appear. In the home the young adolescent, conscious of his/her body, dresses and undresses in privacy. Parents are invited to comment on dress and appearance and notice is taken of parental remarks. Girls seek advice from mothers and test their appearance with fathers: boys do the opposite. There is a lot of teasing between brothers and sisters, and sex in all its connotations forms the background of the young adolescent's life.

Sometimes the incest taboo is not preserved and the young adolescent, particularly the girl, is subjected to the advances of the father. Such a situation may occur against the background of marital discord and the absence of sexual intercourse between the parents. In these circumstances the victim may be afraid of confessing to her mother, not only in order to protect her father but to avoid making the marital situation worse. If a young adolescent who has experienced incest is taken into care, those looking after her have multiple responsibilities. They have to ensure that the young person does not lose sight of the goodness of sex and that the relationship with father—who is often a deprived man of rather limited intelligence—is repaired. The way this matter is handled is important. Constant and repetitious questioning does very little good. The adolescent needs to speak about her experiences once or twice, and these revelations must be received with care. The listening adult must not be shocked nor sexually titillated by the revelations, which need to be treated objectively. The parent's behaviour has to be understood as sad, springing from deprivation rather than an attempt at sexual exploitation, and any good rapport between the two strengthened. Any residual fears about sex need to be listened to with care and sympathy and the goodness of sex as a source of love and creation emphasized.

The importance of sexual attraction as an experience of love needs clarifying. We have seen that the child's experience of love so far depends on its feelings of being recognized, wanted and appreciated for its own sake, and it experiences these feelings in relationships of intimacy and trust where they are present. After puberty, love is denoted in new terms. Now adolescents are said to fall in love, that is to say to feel recognized, wanted and appreciated for their sexual significance. A great deal of confusion is centred on the use of the word love in these two distinct meanings. This confusion is, in fact, widespread in society. Love is in fact described by some entirely in terms of vision, sound and touch of an erotic type, whilst others talk about love in terms of the affection exchanged between parents and child.

The ability to be conscious of both types and harmonize both experiences is the challenge of adolescence. It is a challenge which has a peculiarly Christian dimension. In the past Christianity was extremely chary of the erotic and therefore puberty and adolescence were periods of particular anxiety. The Christian community had no positive meaning for sexuality and therefore all it could say about this period was to admonish the young and forbid the behaviour they most liked to engage in.

Such prohibitions were absolute codes of behaviour. The 'good' young man treated the young girl with decorum and purity. He did not see her in lascivious terms; he did not touch her erotically and he murmured sweet innocent remarks in her ears. Above all, sexual play and intercourse were forbidden. The young lady had to dress with due care and attention. She was not to lead a young man on and not to indulge in erotic play. And once again she had to refuse sexual intercourse. The emphasis on female virginity was paramount.

Unfortunately, even in those eras of strict sexual behaviour, there were double standards and boys were allowed a much greater flexibility than girls. If these prohibitions were questioned, the ultimate answer was that sexual intercourse and its accompanying pleasure were primarily for procreation, which was only appropriate within marriage. Even in the days prior to widespread contraception, the reasons given for the forbidding of sexual enjoyment in adolescence were seriously questioned. Now, however, that contraception has given—theoretically at least—a protection against procreation, Christianity has been deprived of its most compelling answer.

Why should young people not indulge in sexual pleasure and even intercourse provided that procreation is avoided? Christianity has not given a confident answer to this question, and a permissive attitude has swept through society in the last twenty years. This ideology has confidently asserted that, provided no one is hurt, sexual activity in all its forms should not only be indulged in but actually encouraged. What is the Christian answer? Has the time come when the disapproval of fornication is to become obsolete, now that the risk of procreation and illegitimacy have been greatly reduced? Some Christians have argued that, despite contraception, pregnancy and abortion still flourish and that the withdrawal of the fear of pregnancy has had disastrous consequences. This assertion may be true for the community as a whole where free sexual activity has been more widespread than the cautious use of contraceptives. But that is not a satisfactory answer, for there are many individual men and women who do use contraceptives and for whom pregnancy does not follow. Are they behaving in a truly Christian way?

My answer is definitely No, but for different reasons than those given in the past. I do not believe that the instruction to avoid fornication revolves primarily on the matter of procreation. It is true that a baby needs the love of both parents; but it can survive without the presence of both, if needs be. My case rests on the basis that, when bodies encounter each other, ultimately it is persons who meet in intimacy, and both forms of love—that is to say affection and eroticism—should be present.

I believe that when adolescents come together, they are attracted primarily by erotic considerations; but the need for trust, security and the feelings of being recognized, wanted and appreciated are just as important ingredients which need to be present. I believe that sexual intercourse is the sign that both erotic and personal love are present, and the two are united by the seal of intercourse. Normally it is in marriage when the couple have tested in courtship both forms of love that the two are discovered in sufficient strength. I believe that erotic activity and intercourse, isolated from personal love, is in human terms an incomplete experience and its unacceptability for Christians is based on the requirements for authenticity and integrity in the human encounter.

We can see the total dissociation between the two forms of love in the encounter between the prostitute and her client, where only bodies meet and little else. It is true that more and more affection enters as the relationship deepens, and ultimately the criterion by which any sexual activity has to be judged is the presence of both forms of love. In theory this progression should occur in a well tested relationship which culminates in marriage. Sexual intercourse therefore should not be used as an instrument of discovering love but should be the means of sealing its presence, and later on we shall see what further meaning it has in marriage.

Such an approach to adolescent sexuality is extremely demanding. Those who have charge of young people must remember that the principles by which they should live their lives are not easily discerned. Young people will make many mistakes as they have done throughout the ages, but that is no reason to deny the human integrity from which Christian principles follow. In practice young people need a lot of help to come to understand and appreciate these ideas. Only a continuity of the meaning of love in its different stages is likely to be effective in bridging these two different experiences of love.

Masturbation—Single and Together

One of the earliest manifestations of puberty is the desire to masturbate. This is a common experience in boys and increasing in frequency in girls. It is a behaviour which causes embarrassment to adults and a great deal of confusion in young people unless it is handled with care and tact.

The traditional moral stance on masturbation in Christian circles has been to view it with horror and apprehension. The reason for this attitude has been the general disquiet whenever sexual pleasure is experienced and the specific conviction that sexual pleasure is implicitly linked with procreation and belongs to marriage only. Thus many people have grown up in the past with a pronounced sense of guilt associated with masturbation, a guilt which also spreads to other sexual activity. In addition to this type of sexual guilt there were still remnants of past misconceptions which linked masturbation with all sorts of diseases and even insanity.

In the light of all this confusion, what is a modern and reasonable Christian attitude? I believe that masturbation in adolescence is a way by which young people become acquainted with their bodies as sexual entities. It is a way of discovering that they are sexual persons and that sexuality belongs to them. They are not ready for marriage or sexual intercourse and so the morals that apply to that category of behaviour are not applicable. I would, therefore, put forward the view that masturbation is in no way sinful in this phase of development. There are, however, Christian traditions—for example the Roman Catholic one—which still considers masturbation wrong, and this view must be respected. However, even in this tradition the gravity of the sin has been greatly reduced and there is no reason whatsoever to associate masturbation with excessive guilt or apprehension.

Given these moral stances which taken together indicate that masturbation is either no sin at all or, at most, a slight one, how should this behaviour be dealt with in practice?

Even before the boy masturbates he may find himself having what is called a 'wet dream', which means that he has had a spontaneous orgasm. This is an intensely pleasurable experience but may also be frightening. The young person does not understand immediately what is happening to him. If the relationship between himself and his parents or those in charge is good, there is an opportunity for him to approach an adult and ask questions. If he does so then he is given the explanation that this event is nature's way of releasing sexual tension accompanied by pleasure and that it is good and normal.

In due course this spontaneous orgasm will be brought within the control of the young person. The boy will manipulate his penis and the girl her clitoris. The resultant orgasm in the boy will be associated with an ejaculation of sperm which will stain pyjamas or sheets and the observant grown-up will become aware of the masturbating activity of the young person. If the person in charge, be he staff or parent, becomes aware that the child is masturbating, should he confront him? It all depends on the relationship that exists between the two: if there is good rapport and possibly an appropriate background of sexual education, then an explorative conversation may be helpful, evaluating what interest the boy has in this matter. Any anxiety can be met with reassurance and any guilt with appropriate explanation. If the young person shows no interest, then the matter can be left alone and tackled as a group exercise, where adolescent sexual behaviour can be examined in its various aspects.

In tackling the subject of masturbation it is essential to realize that it may be indulged in for various reasons. Most commonly the adolescent will masturbate with sexual fantasies of the opposite sex. These are intensely private experiences which may arise spontaneously or they may be associated with the perusal of sexually explicit or pornographic material. In fact, the discovery of such material may cause a good deal of upset to the staff or parents.

If the link between pornography and masturbation is established, there is need again to treat the association with care and tact. It can be pointed out that the sexual excitation aroused by pictures is understandable at this age but pornographic pictures are a distortion of real people. Real men and women are infinitely more rewarding as sources of genuine love. More often the walls of boys' bedrooms may be plastered with pictures of naked women or those of girls' with popular heroes of screen and music. It is natural that nakedness may be a disturbing sight to those in charge. Adolescent boys have to be helped all the time to realize that real women are much more fun than distorted and exaggerated pictures of naked females. And yet, as the impersonal is rightly criticized, no attempt should be made to deny the fact that the pictures are stimulating. The good sense of those who are guiding young people sexually will only be acknowledged and appreciated if the young person's experience is not denied. Instead it should be constantly added to and widened. Yes, nakedness is exciting. Yes, the desire to look is exciting. Yes, the desire to masturbate with such fantasies is powerful. But all the time the superiority of real flesh and blood should be asserted and the young person pointed in the direction of ultimate reality. A combination of good humour, tact and honesty, always stressing the content of love, brings young people through this phase without shock or shame.

Masturbation may be indulged in as a sort of comfort to get off to sleep. In particular for deprived, tense or inhibited youngsters, the act is a private pleasure which soothes and gives temporary relief to an otherwise isolated and tense experience of life. Such a youngster may turn to masturbation as a way out of intolerable loneliness. In this instance masturbation may be frequent and become a sort of obsession which persists as the young person finds it difficult to mix with others, particularly with members of the opposite sex. Such a lonely youth may, in fact, rely on sex for some pleasure but may also feel very guilty about such behaviour. If such anxieties are brought out in private conversation,

42

reassurance should be given and every encouragement to break the isolation should be made available.

Sometimes masturbation between boys is mutual. A younger boy may be initiated by an older adolescent or even an adult. In these circumstances the younger person may not fully appreciate the meaning of the act and be frightened at the same time that he is excited by it. If boys are caught mutually masturbating each other, once again a great deal of care needs to be shown so that they are not alarmed or frightened by the deed.

Above all, in all private or public talks, it should be stressed that masturbation is a transient experience and will ultimately give way to intercourse in the permanent relationship called marriage.

There are people who have not managed to shed the habit of masturbation in adult life. For some of them the act becomes an obsession which they would like to give up but cannot. They feel trapped in masturbatory activity and they project their concern by warning young people of the dire consequences of starting the habit. These men are totally unsuitable to advise young people, and care should be taken that the sexual education of adolescents does not fall into their hands.

Masturbation is an event to be neither encouraged nor associated with dire warnings. It is a transient activity in the life of the adolescent on the way to reaching and achieving sexual intercourse in marriage. It has its own rhythm for every young boy or girl. For some it is an incessant necessity, for some it is a casual, rare activity, while others never indulge. Whatever its form, it should be associated with affirmative feelings about sex and seen as nature's and God's way to reveal by stages the full plan of sexual activity. In so far as it introduces young people to the mystery of sex, masturbation should not be surrounded by negativity, inhibition and/or guilt. Rather it should be treated as a means to an end, the end being adult sexuality situated in love.

8

Experimenting with Sex

Masturbatory activity is limited to one's own body. Fantasy allows the adolescent to go beyond the body and imagine the beauty and excitation of the opposite sex. In fantasy everything is possible. Boys imagine girls and girls picture boys and in this way the barrier of reality is crossed. But fantasy is not enough. There is an urgent need to discover friendship and sexual reality and adolescents are longing for this contact.

First comes friendship. At this stage in sexual development adolescents are discovering that they mean something special to a person of the opposite sex. This attraction is situated in the body. Girls will take infinite pains with their hair-style, dress, shoes, make-up and boys similarly with their appearance. There is an urge to be recognized now, not only as a person but as a sexual being.

The uncertainty of this phase of development throws girls and boys into peer groups together.There is talk about conquests and for periods of up to months at a time a particular boy and girl will pair with each other. This exclusiveness is partial and in no way does it approach the exclusiveness of courtship. The pair will often go out together with others but there is an understanding that such a couple have a special—even though temporary—meaning for each other.

Such friendships are transient. They are discussed with parents and/or those *in loco parentis*. A great deal of care will be taken in the preparation for going out, and at this point there may be a clash between generations. The older generation may find a particular style too revealing in girls and will say so. The girls in turn may dismiss such criticism as naive and outdated. The important point in such a discussion is to help adolescents to realize that their bodies carry a pronounced meaning for the opposite sex and at the same time to understand how to surround this meaning positively. In other words, the adolescent needs to be encouraged to feel attractive, for attractiveness is neither bad nor evil; it is God's way of bringing about a natural togetherness.

What worries those in charge of adolescents is how to encourage interaction between the sexes without unleashing sexual promiscuity. In the past this was done by being negative and inhibiting regarding sexual attraction. Today such an approach is no longer considered appropriate. But does this mean encouragement should be given to sexual playfulness and activity?

A good deal of clear thinking is needed in this matter. Let us look at what is actually happening inside the world of the two sexes. As far as the boy is concerned, there is an intense physical drive which longs for sexual touch, sexual tension and its release. The boy looks at a girl and is fascinated by her body, which is a powerful source of erotic attraction. Initially looking appears enough, but gradually there is a longing to touch and to explore sexually.

The girl is also attracted by the appearance of a boy and finds his physical features highly exciting. She too longs for touch but, in her case, this is a romantic touch of affection. Traditionally it is the girl who is supposed to have greater control over her sexual feelings and is meant to check the boy's behaviour.

The question that everybody wants the answer to is, what is the appropriate behaviour in this phase of sexual development. In moral terms the question is put in starkest terms; that is, how far should one go in sexual experimenting?

In the past morality used to divide the body into zones; the point of separation was the belt, with the implication that what happened above the belt was acceptable and what happened below was not. This is a very crude and unsatisfactory way of establishing norms for sexual behaviour.

At this stage of sexual attraction boys and girls have an urgent need to be together and a good deal of the sexual interest is focussed on this togetherness. To be taken out to a party, cinema or concert or to go on an outing are all important experiences. This togetherness matters very much and should not be ignored. It applies to both girls and boys, who long to feel that they matter to somebody of the opposite sex. This mutual significance continues from early puberty until the adolescents leave school. It is a time which is principally devoted to learning that one has acquired a sexual significance.

Beyond this sexual significance a couple will also want to discover something about each other's body. The boy will want to kiss. Kissing can be a simple peck or it can involve the mouth as an area of deep sexual contact with its soft, smooth surface which gives a special erotic feel. After the mouth the boy will desire to touch, stroke, caress the breasts of a girl. He will also find her bottom and her thighs attractive. She in turn may find the feeling of being in his arms, kissed and caressed sexually exciting. Finally, there may be genital arousal with the desire for orgasmic relief. How much of all this is appropriate?

In the past there was a rough and ready rule that whatever led ultimately to genital pleasure and arousal was forbidden because this experience led to sexual intercourse, which belonged to marriage alone. This is a view which still prevails in the Roman Catholic tradition and should be respected in those who adhere to this position.

But there are alternative ways of looking at sexual behaviour in adolescence. Just as with masturbation boys and girls discover a part of their sexual potential, so with adolescent experimentation they are discovering something more about each other, from the angle of both affection and—far more important—of erotic awareness. This is the time that God has implanted in our being to discover partially our bodies, a discovery which involves the body as a whole in sexual pleasure. If we accept that erotic pleasure has a meaning of its own, in other words as a body language which is inviting adolescents to become acquainted with it, then there is a place for it without its being wrong.

But what about genital arousal? What about sexual intercourse? I believe that sexual intercourse is the culmination and sealing of a sexual and personal relationship of love. It is not primarily a means of discovering whether two people are suited to each other. It is in fact a powerful expression of love and belongs to a relationship where the commitment of love is appropriately high. This commitment of love has to be no less than lifelong and therefore coitus belongs to marriage.

But actual sexual behaviour is not as clearcut as is depicted in these pages. There is a grey area between sexual play, genital arousal and actual intercourse. Young people, in the course of experimenting with one another, will in fact experience orgasm spontaneously or they may induce it manually in themselves. When this happens, the sexual activity has plainly gone beyond simple sexual exploration. Millions of young people have, in fact, experienced this stage in their sexual experimentation. It does not bring the end of the world. The heavy retribution that was forthcoming in the past whenever genital pleasure was experienced is no longer appropriate because such pleasure has a meaning of its own. It is usually teaching both sexes something fundamental about their bodies and the way they react. Such pleasure of sexual arousal belongs both to intercourse and to spontaneous experience in sexual experimentation. The crucial point is to discuss and explain this principle to a young person. Genital pleasure is part of sexual arousal and ultimately it is part of the culmination of coitus. It bridges the worlds of sexual friendship on the one hand and marriage on the other. Ideally and morally the conduct of the couple should be confined to sexual pleasure in general and not to genital pleasure, which should not be pursued lest it leads to coitus, which definitely belongs to a permanent relationship.

It can be seen that adults discussing this phase with adolescents should be clear in their own minds what principles they are establishing, namely that this is the time for adolescents to get to know each other and the way their bodies respond to sexual arousal. In so far as general sexual pleasure is informing these areas, then it is good and belongs appropriately to this encounter. When it extends to genital pleasure then it belongs partially to this phase and ultimately to marriage. A certain amount of overlap is inevitable but it does finally express the seal to a permanent relationship and, if viewed in this manner, should not be pursued for its own sake until the love present in the relationship requires the genital union which belongs only to a final commitment in marriage.

These are the principles; what about their application?

Generally adolescents pursue their sexual life in silence and isolation. Adults are not confident enough to go into details, but that is not an acceptable excuse. Both in individual counselling and in group teaching adolescents need to know and understand both how their bodies function and what meaning they have for the opposite sex. By now it is vital that the biology of sexual function is understood and that the ingredients which make up fertilization are clear. There is no excuse for pregnancies which are based on ignorance of how babies are conceived. Equally, adolescents—particularly girls—need to appreciate psychologically the impact their bodies have on boys and to be helped to understand the needs and make-up of their particular friend.

This outline applies to the average boy and girl between the age of twelve and leaving school. But even during this period there will be some youngsters who are particularly vulnerable and who find it difficult to mix in ordinary social exchanges. There will be young girls who are so shy that they find it very difficult to mix with boys. They will be most reluctant to dress and go out to mixed parties because they are convinced that they are not attractive enough. If they go to a party, they will stand aloof because they are afraid to be befriended. If a boy makes a gesture towards them, they will be reluctant to respond. Adolescents of both sexes may be plagued with acne or with some other real or imaginary physical distortion, expect rejection and be reluctant to risk it. These vulnerable young people need extra support and encouragement. They need special attention to remind them that they are attractive and desirable in their own right.

Some girls may have experienced sexual traumas in earlier years such as incest, rape or other sexual episodes. They may be particularly sensitive to going out with boys, afraid that they will be hurt again. Once again such people need special reassurance that they have to trust anew in the hope and conviction that their new experiences will be good ones.

At the other end of the scale there will be girls and boys who appear promiscuous. The girls are ready to give their sexual favours indiscriminately and the boys will boast proudly of their conquests. Such youngsters need particular understanding. Behind this rush of sexual activity may be profound fears that nobody really wants them. There may be long histories of deprivation and emotional need in their past. Sexual activity offers these people the feeling of being wanted. In fact the actual sexual experience may be of limited interest to the person concerned. Sexual attraction is a means of obtaining the attention which is desperately needed. This need is so urgent that anyone who can provide it is instantly approved of. The result is that relationships change rapidly and the only thing that matters is that someone should be available. The frequency of change, coupled with the overt sexual interest, gives these youngsters the character of promiscuity, but often these young men and women are really emotionally impoverished and are desperately seeking attention from any quarter.

It is easy to indict such persons with sexual irresponsibility. On the surface they appear to be totally wrapped up with themselves and their current friends. Inside, these youngsters are vulnerable, easy prey to rejection, to mood swings, to disappointment and hurt. It is vital that every attempt should be made to reach them and look beyond their sexual adventures. They often appear to be completely out of control, and yet what they need is an enormous amount of personal attention. They need to be helped to understand that sex is exciting, attractive and good but what they are seeking is a personal commitment and acceptance which sex alone can never give.

Not all boys and girls who are preoccupied with sexual interest are deprived individuals. There are some youngsters who get an enormous amount of fun by being flirtatious. Such an approach to sex must not be condemned provided that the expectations do not exceed the possibilities present. Sex alone will not solve all the problems of adolesence. These young men and women still have to complete their studies and prepare for work. The magic belief that a relationship with a boy or a girl solves all of life's problems has to be corrected. There are no short-cuts to wholeness.

In fact, adolescence is a difficult period in which to achieve wholeness. Up to the period of puberty the child was learning the meaning of love through its relationships with adults. Now there is a need to learn the meaning of the body as a sexual organ and as a source of powerful attraction. In due course these two dimensions of love will have to be fused, but the time is not yet ripe.

For the time being the adolescent is learning through experiment to be aware of his/her body. This body is a source of excitement and pleasure, and there is a tremendous temptation to isolate the bodily experience and to pursue it on its own. This path must be avoided and the task of those in charge of young people at this time of their lives is to help them appreciate that sexual attraction and pleasure are good but have a further purpose which is to bring couples together in permanent relationships where love and sex unite.

9

Premarital Sex—Contraception, Pregnancy and Abortion

At this point it is worth repeating the principles with which to judge adolescent sexual behaviour. Traditionally fornication has been forbidden for two reasons. The first is that all forms of sexual pleasure belong to marriage; the second that the primary purpose of sexual intercourse is procreation, which belongs to marriage. So for these two reasons all sexual intercourse was forbidden prior to marriage.

In this book it has been argued that a generalized sexual pleasure flowing from heterosexual attraction and awareness of each other's bodies belongs properly to adolescence, when young people have to become acquainted with their bodies. This idea is certainly likely to raise some criticism, but it flows from my belief that God has implanted certain sexual feelings in our bodies which we are meant to discover at the appropriate time, which happens to be in adolescence. So that it is natural for young people to wish to meet, enjoy each other's company, receive pleasure and joy from their bodies with some inevitable genital tension. But this tension is not to be a prelude to sexual intercourse. Sexual intercourse is not a part of this adolescent discovery; it is clearly the seal of a love between two people who have reached the stage of life commitment and are ready to raise children in the permanent union which we call marriage.

Nevertheless we know that premarital sexual intercourse may occur and it is necessary to understand its characteristics. There are those who insist that sexual intercourse has nothing to do with love: it is simply a source of genital pleasure and should be pursued for its own sake. This is a view of coitus which is basically inhuman and certainly not Christian. When bodies meet, so do persons and, in order for the exchange to be fully human there has to be a union of affection and genital sex. Affection means the presence of trust, security, the knowledge of feeling recognized, wanted and appreciated and the possibility of continuity and reliability. These aspects of affection grow as a relationship deepens and finally meet in a permanent commitment we call marriage. When sexual intercourse is separated from affection it is incomplete and takes place with selfish designs of purely personal satisfaction with little care of what happens to the other person.

The other person who runs the greatest risk is the girl who can become pregnant. It is the girl who has to be safeguarded. The best safeguard is the training which makes it absolutely clear that intercourse is the seal of love of a permanent relationship and should only take place in marriage.

Most girls will appreciate this precept and will not engage in promiscuous intercourse. But some will; as already mentioned, these are young women with deprived, rejected backgrounds who long for affection, or what they think is affection, and are prepared to have sex as the price to be paid for getting attention. These girls have to be protected from themselves, and those in charge, be they parents or parent substitutes, have a grave responsibility towards them.

A common-sense view is to encourage these girls to use contraceptives, but such an action is fraught with moral dilemmas. First of all, there are the traditions such as the Roman Catholic one which forbid their use and this is a factor to be considered when the person belongs to that faith. When no such moral issues exist, there is another dilemma which comes down to the fact that, if girls are encouraged to use contraceptives, is this not a way of saying to them that they should indulge in intercourse? Clearly the indiscriminate encouragement of contraceptives as a way of facilitating safe intercourse has no place in any home or organization with Christian beliefs about the proper place of intercourse within marriage.

Nevertheless it is inevitable that a children's home or an ordinary family will be faced with the individual girl who has made it abundantly clear that she intends to have sexual intercourse. What is the responsible adult attitude then?

Those who see in contraception an evil have to choose between this evil and the damage of a pregnancy. Those who do not see contraception as an evil have also to decide whether its use may encourage further sexual intercourse as well as prevent a possible pregnancy. If a girl is determined to have intercourse, whatever anyone says, then clearly her protection from a pregnancy becomes a vital issue and, provided her conscience and those of her advisers do not object to contraception, it should be used.

Here, some would object that all the emphasis is being placed on the girl. What about the boy? Should he not be held responsible for the consequences of his sexual activity? The answer is of course he should and, if he too is determined to have intercourse irrespective of all the advice given to the contrary, then common sense dictates that he should become responsible for his action. Nevertheless, when adolescents become involved in determined sexual activity, their responsibility does not always match their actions and, since it is the girl who has to bear the burden of the pregnancy, the most serious thought has to be directed towards her protection.

What happens if the girl does become pregnant? Unfortunately this does happen. Clearly the choice is between the continuation of the pregnancy and a termination. As far as Christian principles are concerned, I believe that I am expressing the united Christian opinion that abortion is not consistent with either human or Christian principles, which emphasize the preservation of life and not its destruction. This is a view that antedated Christianity and is to be found in the very origins of Greek medicine in the Hippocratic oath, which forbade abortion. Life is a gift, a precious gift from God, and everything should be done to preserve it so that, when facing the alternatives of continuing a pregnancy or terminating it, the Christian answer must always be on behalf of life.

If the decision is taken to continue with the pregnancy, then clearly the girl involved needs to be supported fully. In the past the presence of a pregnancy meant that everyone wanted the girl to marry the boy concerned and pressure was put on her to achieve this end. We now know that such marriages run a great risk of breakdown later on and should not be pursued unless there is a genuine affection and desire to marry.

That means that the girl—who can still be at school—needs all the protection and support she can get from those around her. Despite the circumstances of its origin, a pregnancy is still the occasion of the miracle of life and such a young mother needs to be encouraged to rejoice in her maternity. There is no room for investing her with guilt or badness and certainly no place for judgements and/or rejection. Judgement belongs to God alone and so does condemnation. Ours is a task of loving and helping the girl to cherish her baby. There are both practical and emotional aspects of encouragement and, above all, it is vital that the experience should leave no trauma in her life. This is the time when she needs companionship, the opportunity to talk about her feelings regarding the pregnancy and encouragement to spell out her fears so that they can be allayed.

Finally, the baby will arrive and its future will have to be decided. Those in charge of the girl's life think of the burden and responsibility that a baby creates and are busy planning its adoption. This plan of action may coincide with the girl's own wishes; but it may not. A deprived girl may find that this is her first opportunity to call someone her own, to be responsible for its life and to lavish love on it. When everybody else is thinking of the problems, the girl is obsessed with the opportunity of loving and is determined not to let go. One sees and admires these young girls who take on the responsibility of motherhood and battle successfully alone. Clearly they deserve all the help they can be given, and the Christian community has the responsibility of supporting them fully. If the decision is made to place the baby in care or for adoption, then the girl's sense of loss and mourning has to be taken into account. She has nurtured the baby for nine months and it has become part of herself. In giving it up, she is giving up part of herself and there is inevitable grief and distress at the loss. This distress should be appreciated and treated sympathetically.

Sometimes the girl may experience a depressive reaction following the birth of her baby, and if it is severe it may need psychiatric intervention. But most women suffer a transient period of the blues which then clear up without further trouble.

It is imperative that a girl's decision about the future of the pregnancy be taken seriously. Often the girl will opt for the continuation of the pregnancy, but some may decide in favour of a termination. Such a decision should not be the result of coercion from parents or those in charge. As already stated, a termination is never the primary choice for a Christian. But in the world of the wounded human personalities who become pregnant, there is not always sufficient strength to accept the responsibility of carrying on with the pregnancy. If, in fact, a girl chooses a termination and if it is refused by those in charge, she may in fact try to abort herself or land in unscrupulous hands that may make a terrible mess of terminating. If for some reason a termination is decided upon, then it should be carried out in a proper hospital setting which will ensure that no damage occurs to the female organs involved.

After a termination the girl may feel guilty and may be weighed down both by the moral consequences of her action and the sense of psychological loss of her baby. She may need proper spiritual support and also some counselling to regain her sense of confidence and self-esteem.

Whether a girl has decided in favour of remaining pregnant or of termination, she needs the continuous encouragement and support of those around her. In the past such girls were given asylum but treated as if they were sexual lepers. We can do no better than remind ourselves that Jesus Christ mixed with prostitutes and women with other sexual problems. He never approved of sexual sin but equally never rejected the sinner. It is vital that young people who become sexually involved in intercourse, pregnancy and/or a termination should not be damaged as persons. Those responsible for them must exercise patience, compassion and genuine love. These youngsters have to face a life of marriage with further intercourse and pregnancy, and nothing should be said or done which limits their future capacity to enter fully into these experiences and engage lovingly in them.

Finally, a word should also be said about venereal disease. If boys and girls engage in sexual intercourse they can certainly become infected. It is important that the atmosphere of a home should be such that there is sufficient trust for a young person to confide to those in charge and seek help. Nowadays help is in plentiful supply and should be sought without delay. Once again a boy or girl in this predicament should be treated lovingly and the condition kept a secret if that is possible.

10

Living Together

For over sixty years there have been advocates who have recommended living together as an alternative to marriage or as a preliminary to it. For a long time such an idea had no great attraction, but currently there are young people who are practising it. I want to look at its meanings, both overt and hidden; its place in our society and its Christian implications.

In theory a couple who live together have the freedom to try out an intimate life without exclusive commitments towards each other. They enjoy the privilege of a social, emotional, sexual, intellectual and spiritual life together. They find out whether they are suited to each other, and this trial may last for months or sometimes years.

It is perfectly true that on the surface a couple appear to enjoy all the experiences of life as if they were married. At the social level they find out their common interests, what they like doing together and what separately. In particular they have a chance to discover how much time they want to be in each other's company and how much on their own. They have a chance to find out whether their partners' needs are so demanding that there is not enough time for themselves, or whether they are jealous of each other's friendships. If they do experience jealousy, they may have quarrels with each other which test their trust and faithfulness. There are other daily events which are tested, such as how much contribution each makes to the household and whether they can organize their life together at the level of actually managing a household. Frequently a couple living together will not have children and so they will be likely to be both working, which means that money will not be in short supply, but they will have an opportunity to find out how they manage money together. In particular the man will find out whether the woman is a good housekeeper and she whether he can manage money efficiently. They may agree to handle money jointly and this will be a good test for mutual trust and power-sharing.

At the emotional level such a couple will test their ability to communicate with each other. Communication is much more than the exchange of words. It requires the ability to listen carefully to what another person is saying in terms of meaning. Words are not always available to convey adequately different moods and feelings and so, in listening to each other, a couple have to learn to be sensitive to the nuances and secret messages. In particular they have to learn whether both are capable of communicating sufficiently with each other. Often women are much better at expressing their feelings than men and they get upset when their men will not talk to them about *their* feelings. In this trial period the couple can learn to respond accurately to each other's needs.

The fact that a couple live together will not spare them from having arguments and quarrels. When they do quarrel they have a chance to find out how quickly they can make it up. Most couples agree to forgive and forget quickly. But there are men and women who cannot do so. They withdraw in a huff and sulk for hours, sometimes days or even weeks. This response to conflict may be so important that it can undermine their life together.

Beyond communication and conflict at the emotional level, a couple have to find out how comfortable they are with each other at the level of dependence and independence; that is to say to what extent one partner depends on the other emotionally for initiative, decision-making, policy-making, nurturing and generally behaving as a parental figure. Such emotional dependence may suit a couple excellently at the beginning of their living together, but years later, when they have married, the dependent partner outgrows the dependency and also outgrows the other partner. In this respect the trial marriage is not a very good experiment to find out whether a couple are suited together because the ultimate test of suitability is not going to emerge until some time later on.

Another dimension of suitability is that of activity and

passivity. Here is another example where initially a couple may complement each other in this respect. One partner, who may be of either sex, appears to be the assertive one, showing all the signs of being the extrovert person. The other is happy to let the assertive person take charge and remains passive.

The assertive person appears to be in charge instinctually, emotionally and socially. That is to say, he/she initiates sexual activity, expresses affection with words and actions and is the lively one in social situations. The passive partner appears to be happy to follow suit and respond to the lead given by the partner. Such a combination appears to be comfortable and suitable but it can also be misleading. It can be misleading because behind the initiator and assertive personality there may be unconsciously a great need to be looked after, and in fact there are moments when such a person longs to become passive and be taken care of. This need may emerge whilst the couple are living together, but in fact it takes extra stress such as having a child, an illness or a loss before this side of the personality shows itself and this revelation may not take place until years later or when the couple have married. So once again the trial period may not be such a reliable test as it first appears.

A third area is the amount of time spent together and separate. It is obvious that a couple living together will spend as much time together as possible. They are drawn together by emotional and sexual feelings and they find it very difficult to visualize being separated. And yet they have not experienced the testing time when there are children and the mother feels trapped whilst the husband can escape to the pub, the soccer field, work or other forms of activity. Thus once again living together is not the ideal testing time that it is supposed to be.

The case that is being made out in this chapter is that, whilst on the surface a couple may appear to be experiencing a full life together, in practice there are a number of factors which make living together different from marriage.

So far I have mentioned some of the emotional changes that occur in the course of time and cannot be anticipated by living together. There are, however, other reasons which make living together an even less reliable guide to the future.

59

Some couples come to live together as an escape from an unhappy home. All they want is the immediate warmth, security and acceptance of each other. They value these experiences so much that they ignore all their differences. They live in an ideal world where they feel loved, and this is all that concerns them. In due course this ideal world will dissolve into everyday experiences and then the real test of suitability will emerge.

By far the most important objection psychologically to living together is the fact that the couple are not securely committed to each other. They know that they are on trial and without realizing it they only show that part of themselves which they feel will be acceptable. They know that they can be repudiated and they do not have the safety and security to be themselves. Unconsciously they hold back parts of themselves which they fear and in particular they will not be angry or make scenes about issues which they do not feel absolutely safe.

In practice a couple will decide to marry when they are contemplating having a baby or when they think that the time has come to convert their relationship into a permanent one. This may be a combined decision but it may be the wish of one partner only. The other party may in fact resist converting the relationship into a permanent one. People with this attitude may be conscious that they enjoy the freedom of an uncommitted relationship, or in fact they may unconsciously fear that if they marry they will feel trapped. So that one of the reasons for not getting married is the very fear of being committed. This fear may in fact be a very powerful one and responsible for a good deal of the resistance to actual marriage.

The time will come for marriage and in practice it is found that some couples begin to have difficulties from the very day that they get married. It is not unusual for couples to complain that at the very moment when they get married their sexual life becomes disturbed, their conflicts escalate and their peace is shattered. It is abundantly clear that in these situations the living together was a protection against the difficulties that emerge when the couple commit themselves fully to marriage.

The reason often given for a couple's living together is

that, if they are in love with each other, a ceremony in church or a piece of paper in the registry office will not alter their feelings for each other. Once again this reasoning has surface value, and yet the Christian answer is that a couple need a full and public ceremony in order to be truly married. Why does Christianity adopt this attitude?

There are historic reasons in favour of a public church ceremony. In the Middle Ages it was possible to be validly married in the eyes of the Church privately if a couple promised to take each other as husband and wife and live together as such. These unions were the equivalent of the living together of today and were called clandestine marriages carried out in private. The same arguments were offered in favour of these alliances as are offered today. The trouble was that these private vows could be and were repudiated. Women found themselves married and abandoned and men committed themselves privately to more than one woman. The need for a public witness became vital.

But these historic reasons are not the only ones. A marriage is both a private commitment and a public event. Society is involved when a couple marry. The couple are no longer free to be courted by anyone else. They gather rights to themselves as married people; they own property and they become the parents of children. In all these areas society is involved in being a public witness to the marriage and also in supporting it in various ways. Furthermore, Christianity lays great stress on a permanent and exclusive commitment as being proper to marriage. It is only in the presence of a permanent commitment that the couple have the freedom to look at their disappointments, conflicts, differences of opinion without the fear of losing their partners. The vows taken publicly have the strength of reminding the couple when they are at their lowest that they are committed to each other and somehow they have to find an answer to their worst troubles. For many people the commitment of permanency which Christianity requires for marriage appears to suggest that Christianity condemns the married to a sentence of life imprisonment. It is in fact nothing of the sort. It is exactly the other way round. Christianity demands a permanent commitment which is both private and public because this is the strongest human guarantee that we

61

possess which can safeguard the vicissitudes of a human relationship as complicated as marriage.

Nevertheless, up to fifteen per cent of couples live together for longer or shorter periods. For them economic and ideological reasons are compelling and they decide to challenge the mores of society. In fact society is much more lenient towards couples living together than ever before.

But what about the attitudes of parents or those who have been in charge before? All sorts of difficulties arise. Perhaps the simplest of all is the correct nomenclature. What does one call a couple living together? We have not devised a name for them. They are not friends, they are not engaged, and they are not married. Most parents resort to calling them by their Christian names. And then when they come to spend the night at home, are they offered one bedroom? One bed? Are they treated as a couple or not? These are the embarrassing situations which face the older generation.

Over and above the practical considerations, what should the attitude of Christians be towards such a couple? There are those who would wish to repudiate and condemn them out of the Christian community. They feel that they have to make a stand against what they consider to be open fornication. There are others who shrug their shoulders and accept the situation as if there was nothing to say.

Both these attitudes lack Christian integrity. There is no doubt at all that the orthodox Christian position should be stated unequivocally. Living together is not the same as marriage and the two should not be confused. The truth as we know it and understand it should be declared. At the same time we should look carefully at the behaviour. If a couple are living together in a committed and exclusive relationship, faithful to one another, they do have a lot of the appropriate attributes present. To that extent we should recognize that the missing elements are important but limited.

In this, as in all situations where the moral law is contravened, we have to be Christ-like and be clear about sin whilst immensely compassionate towards the sinner. In other words, we have to retain an attitude of brotherly love towards such couples so that they can be kept within the confines of the Christian community and not alienated from it. In due course they will wish to get married and, when this happens, one hopes that they will choose a Christian ceremony. Furthermore, when their children are born it is also hoped that they will have them baptized and brought up as Christians.

Living together is an aberrant form of marriage. Despite its similarity to marriage, it is not truly the latter and the Christian community must not be confused by the two. For some couples it is a serious time of preparation for marriage, which when it comes is successful. For others it is an escape from serious commitment rationalized in a variety of ways. In practice the orthodox position should be upheld and, at the same time, the couple treated with compassion and understanding so that the Christian life remains open to them when they feel free to choose it.

11

Sexual Variations

So far all that has been written refers to normal sexual development with heterosexual orientation. It is well known, however, that sexual interest can take different forms. These forms of sexuality have been called in the past deviations, suggesting that they are in fact abnormal variants. Those who have these tendencies decry the label of abnormality. For them their sexual desires are in fact quite normal and they resent the label of deviancy which they feel is a value judgement which is totally unwarranted. There is a strong case to be made to respect this view and to call these tendencies variations; hence the title of this chapter.

In the past and up to a point even today, both society and the Christian community have responded to these tendencies with shock, horror and distinct disapproval. These attitudes have tended to isolate the men and women concerned, who feel ashamed, guilty and on the fringe of the community. Such an attitude is unforgivable and often stems from the sheer ignorance that surrounds these topics. In this chapter I would like to introduce and comment on some of the commonest variations.

Infantile Sexuality
It will be remembered that Freud described an infantile sexuality whereby sexual energy or libido was situated first in the mouth, then in the anus and finally in the genital area with the resolution of various complexes. These sites assume in the post-pubertal period a sexual significance of some importance. As already stated, the mouth is lined with a particular type of skin called the mucous membrane which is exquisitely sensitive, and the mouth and lips assume significance in adult sexuality for kissing and oral sexual stimu-

lation. This form of stimulation may lead to oral intercourse or simply oral stimulation of the genital organs. These practices have been frowned upon and indeed remain unmentionable except in special literature with a pornographic flavour. In view of the widespread nature of oral involvement in sexual stimulation this furtive silence is no longer justified.

What are the moral implications of these activities? There are at least two basic issues involved. The first is that the mouth and lips can enhance sexual excitation and therefore pleasure. Here there is no basic problem except for those who are frightened by the concept of sexual pleasure. Since such pleasure is a gift from God there are no grounds for entertaining any anxiety over it. The second involves the use of the mouth to bring about an orgasm either by licking the vagina or by stimulating the penis in the mouth. Traditional thought prescribes that all sexual activity leading to an orgasm should take place between penis and vagina in order for the semen to be deposited in the vagina, leaving its procreative potential open. This still would be the view of the Roman Catholic Church. For the rest of Christianity, which has accepted artificial contraception, the mouth is an instrument of birth control, although it may not be seen as such by the couple concerned. It is seen as a means of varying sexual fulfilment and as such a source of legitimate pleasure. There is little doubt that many couples enjoy both this form of stimulation and intercourse and find it perfectly acceptable; provided the surrounding aura of horror is removed, there is no reason—conscience permitting—why such activity should not occur.

The same applies to anal stimulation and intercourse. Given the excreting nature of the anus, we tend to surround this orifice with a certain disgust. And yet for some people anal stimulation is pleasurable and so is intercourse. Clearly anal stimulation provides no moral dilemma for those who enjoy it. It is part and parcel of a general enhancement of sexual stimulation. Anal intercourse is a different matter. Once again the traditional Christian teaching would require all intercourse to be a penis-vagina encounter so that procreation remains open. Thus anal intercourse would be forbidden to Roman Catholics. Other traditions, which do not persist with the idea that every sexual act must be open to new life, would not have the same objection. But the law takes a hand here for anal intercourse between husband and wife is illegal. What happens sometimes is that women permit this activity—and even enjoy it—and later on, when the marriage breaks down, use the same activity as a complaint against the husband. The fact is that once again, conscience permitting, anal intercourse may be a variant that enhances the sexual life of a couple.

The third stage of infantile sexuality is the resolution of the Oedipus and Electra complexes. Basically this means that the boy should detach himself from the sexual attraction to mother and the girl likewise from father. If these detachments do not occur, then there is likelihood of failure of sexual and gender maturation; that is, the boy identifying with the maleness of the father and the girl with the femaleness of mother. This concept is important in the next variation, which is homosexuality.

Homosexuality
In the last thirty years the subject of homosexuality has come to the forefront. Numerous books have been published on the subject, and not least amongst them are those which give us an idea of the number of those involved. Since the work of Kinsey we have accepted that the exclusive homosexual may form as much as five per cent of the total male population and two-and-a-half per cent of the female population. In a country like England and Wales this group may amount to about one million men and half a million women, so that it is a sizeable variation. Indeed, in terms of overt sexual behaviour it is probably the commonest.

There is a considerable Christian tradition on homosexuality, mostly hostile. The writings of the Old and the New Testaments rigidly interpreted are very critical of homosexual practices. Recent studies have questioned these strict interpretations but there is no consensus which has emerged yet on this matter. Christian teaching is concerned with active homosexual behaviour, but before this is discussed there is a great deal more that needs attention.

The first point to stress is that homosexuality by itself is another sexual variation and not a sinful state. It is characterized by an emotional and sexual attraction towards a person of the same sex. Homosexuals are men and women who, through no fault of their own, find themselves attracted towards their own sex. They need to form human relationships with friendship and companionship just like everybody else. The response of the Christian community must be to acknowledge that homosexuals are our brothers and sisters in Christ. There is no justification whatsoever for keeping them out of our churches or communities. They need our friendship and love and we owe to them these elementary Christian obligations. This means that we need to open our hearts and homes to them and accept them in our lives on the same basis as our heterosexual friends. These steps do not require any major moral changes, but simply a Christian good will.

Granted that we accept homosexuals as our friends and encourage them to play a major role in Christian and secular life, this is not going to be enough. Homosexual men and women need support, healing and growth in their own lives. They are likely to seek these characteristics from fellow homosexuals. So what should our attitude be to the pairing of homosexuals? I can see no objection to such pairings. Indeed, one would welcome them, particularly if there is stability and commitment in them. They are infinitely preferable to casual, transient encounters and the loneliness of isolated men and women.

Finally what about sexual relations within such relationships? Here the tradition on the whole is against such activity. Indeed, recent pronouncements from the Roman Catholic Church make it abundantly clear that it is forbidden. It will be clear by now that the Roman Catholic Church maintains the strictest sexual discipline, but in the area of homosexuality many other Churches also retain this strict attitude. It is based on two grounds: first, that homosexual activity is immoral in itself and, second, that sexual intercourse is directed towards procreation, impossible for homosexuals.

There are other Churches that take the view that, if homosexuals are to stay together in committed permanent relationships, then sexual intercourse should be permitted because it contributes to the love and stability of the relationship and this is the primary consideration for homosexuals. Clearly, with such a wide range of moral possibilities, homosexuals must plan their own lives in the light of their consciences. What is absolutely clear is that relationship is better than isolation and loneliness: that permanent commitment is better than transient exchanges and that faithfulness is better than promiscuity.

A good deal of homosexuality emerges in adolescence and therefore is particularly pertinent here. The awareness that one is attracted towards one's own sex comes as a shock to many adolescents. They find it difficult to believe it, and yet inwardly they know that they are much happier with their own sex and find heterosexual friendships uninteresting by comparison. It takes time to come to terms with this realization and they need mature and wise parents and counsellors who can help them to accept their state without revulsion or shame. Parents or parent substitutes may be shocked by the revelation that their offspring or charges are homosexual and they may torture themselves about their contribution to the state. They need not suffer unnecessarily. We know very little about what contributes to this variation. Some experts maintain that nurture is the cause and others that it is genetic factors beyond the control of parents or anyone else who is concerned with the upbringing of children. It would be true to say that we do not really know what contributes to the variation and it is likely that more than one factor is responsible.

Beyond the positive acceptance of the state, it is important to remember that not all young people who experience attraction towards their own sex will necessarily finish as exclusive homosexuals. Everybody knows that adolescents may have crushes on members of their own sex at schools or afterwards which are ephemeral and not persistent. Indeed, some experts maintain that no permanent orientation is established until the middle twenties and so great care should be taken not to affix a label too early. If, on the other hand, the tendency is there clearly in interest, attraction, dreams and unconscious orientation, then denial of the obvious is purposeless. Life has to be lived fully in that style.

Bisexuality

The uncertainty of sexual orientation found in adolescence may in fact persist and lead to a condition of bisexuality. Bisexuals are able to have emotional and sexual relationships with both sexes. They may get married, have children and indeed be most successful spouses and parents. Sometimes, however, under stress they shift from their heterosexual connections to homosexual ones. There are men, for example, who marry but when they are depressed, under stress, in marital difficulties, take refuge in homosexual practices. These episodes are transient and offer minor comfort. Occasionally a man or woman may find, in middle life, that bisexuality has been finally converted to full homosexuality, and that is how some marriages break down. Thus for some bisexuals there is a final leaning towards homosexuality later on in life which can have a devastating effect on a marriage.

Cross-dressing

In our modern society we find a certain amount of unisex. By cross-dressing we mean the desire to wear clothing which belongs normally to the opposite sex. This desire can start early and young adolescents, particularly boys, may be found wishing to wear female underclothing. Indeed, some boys get hold of their mothers' underclothing and masturbate with various articles. As they get older they find an increasing instinctual pressure to wear female garments underneath their male ones. There are a number of men who wear female pants, brassieres and other items under their clothing. When a youngster is caught behaving in this way, those apprehending him sometimes feel that they have a sexual monster in their midst. Nothing of the sort is present.

When we look at the development of a boy we realize how intimately connected he is with his mother's body. For a number of years his gratification is found in her arms, on her knees and in the consequent encirclement of his body with female garments. It is not surprising that some boys become attracted not only to mother's body but to her clothes, which now become gratifying in their own right. The boy wishes to retain the link with mother and does so by wearing some of the articles which belong to her. Such an action is both gratifying and comforting simultaneously. The little girl on the other hand does not have to cross-dress. The articles which her mother wears become in due course her normal form of dress; in fact cross-dressing is mainly a male characteristic.

As these transvestites—as they are called—grow up, they desire to dress completely in female clothing and in fact do so in the privacy of their own homes or go out in female dress in the dark. Such cross-dressing can relieve a good deal of instinctual frustration. Transvestites are not homosexuals, and the two variations must not be confused. Transvestites are attracted by women, fall in love with them, marry and father children. Sooner or later their secret of cross-dressing will emerge and their wives will get to know about it. A number of wives find such cross-dressing acceptable and help their husbands with it. Some men like to have sexual inter-course when they are cross-dressed and once again many a wife will tolerate such behaviour. There are men, however, who do not have such co-operative wives and feel obliged to keep their needs secret from them.

Morally speaking cross-dressing does not pose any issues of great importance. If a man wants to cross-dress, there is no earthly reason why he should not. It is a harmless vari-ation and, provided it is acceptable to his wife, it can enhance their married life.

Finally, in the same category as cross-dressing must be added transexuality, which applies to men who not only want to dress as women but want to become women in body. Transexuals are fewer compared to transvestites. They want to have an operation to transform their bodies into female ones. These operations are carried out when a person sat-isfies all the emotional, psychological and sexual criteria of really being born in the 'wrong' form of body. Clearly, if this is the case, then plastic surgery completes what nature has designed. There are famous transexuals who felt they were in the wrong sex since their earliest childhood and only came to a sense of peace when they were operated upon and rendered female.

Rubber and Fur Fetishism
Sometimes men and women can be fascinated sexually by an object or part of the body. These are called fetishes.

Amongst the best known fetishes are rubber and fur. As before it is men far more than women who are fascinated by these objects which stimulate them sexually. Men like to see, touch, stroke rubber or fur. They like in particular their girlfriends to wear such objects and things like rubber mackintoshes can be very sexually exciting. Once again there is no moral problem with fetishism except when the fetish is used in isolation to masturbate. Whilst adolescent masturbation has its own justification, adult sexual activity should be relational and here the fetish may assist in sexual arousal but should not become a substitute for normal sexual intercourse.

Sado-masochism
Undoubtedly the commonest sexual variation is sado-masochism. In sadism gratification is derived from or associated with the infliction of pain. Masochism is the opposite experience, for it is the reception of pain which is sexually stimulating. The origins of sado-masochism are obscure. It is possible that there are painful and pleasurable centres in the brain which are intimately related. It is also possible that as young children receive attention through criticism or punishment, this negative attention becomes a source of pleasure. There are plenty of documented experiences in which childhood physical punishment is associated with pleasure and this type of gratification is clearly wrong. But what about minor forms of sado-masochism mutually realized and experienced by couples for whom it is a mildly stimulating sexual variation? In these circumstances it is permissible because it is experienced in the context of love.

In this chapter only a mere outline of sexual variations has been given, but it can easily be seen that in so far as these variations are learned patterns of behaviour, their roots are to be found in childhood. In this context no home or educational establishment can shut its eyes to the potential origin of these sexual interests. Instead of looking in a different direction, ignoring or taking a severe moral line, it is imperative that we face such behaviour openly, caringly and compassionately. Those who are in the grip of these problems should be encouraged to integrate them in a life of love so

71

that the love of neighbour remains uppermost, and in this way God's presence will be safeguarded.

12

Healing in the Second Decade

The second decade of life is singled out for the emergence of the sexual characteristics of puberty and adult erotic activity. But a great deal more happens during this period. In fact three outstanding features characterize adolescence: namely, the ultimate autonomy from parents in a final phase of separation, the seeking of work and the advent of heterosexual experience. Each of these features is fundamental to the human personality and I would like to look at them more closely.

The ultimate separation at the end of the second decade does not occur for the individual without adequate preparation. Separation begins in the second and third years of life, when the young child learns to do things for itself which hitherto were done by mother. It learns to walk, talk, feed and dress itself and thus gains a measure of instrumental independence. This independence is limited and its next phase comes round about age nine or ten, when the young child looks at parents without a sense of awe and begins to demand justice in the way he or she is treated. The big gap of inequality between parent and child is narrowed, and the young person begins to establish some independence of thinking and acting. It is this independence which continues in the second decade.

The form it takes is social, physical, emotional, intellectual and spiritual. At the social level the young person gradually withdraws from the immediacy of parents. He will slowly abandon going on holidays with them and will go to different places with friends. His friends will be his peers and he will belong to a group or gang. With his associates he will feel at home and the group cohesion gives a strength which he does not have on his own. At the physical level the young person is assuming the definition of a young adult with the sexual features standing out. At the emotional level there is a great deal of autonomy. The young person now begins to feel a person in his own right and is attracted by persons of the opposite sex with whom intimacy is established. In this intimacy, trust, liking, acceptance, availability, rejoicing, gratification and fulfilment are all exchanged. Intellectually the young person can now enter the range of abstract ideas and cross boundaries of imagination and reason hitherto impossible. Finally this is the time when altruistic values ascend to unbelievable heights. The young person can identify with the poor, the needy and the deprived and ultimately with the source of all creation, goodness and love. Whilst the overwhelming majority of young people negotiate these aspects of autonomy there are a number who are handicapped in one or more ways.

In social terms there are young men and women who find it extremely difficult to separate from the physical intimacy of parents. These young persons are frightened to go out and meet other young people. They stay at home and either read, play records or watch television. The step of physically leaving the safety of home causes them acute anxiety which amounts to panic.

These young phobics may stay at home, month in, month out. They still go on holidays and weekly outings with their parents. They find it very difficult to experience the anxiety of physical separation which they dread. These young people need gradual persuading that separation will not be detrimental to their peace of mind. They can be befriended and assisted to come out for walks, entertainment, meetings where they have to meet other people without losing sight of their befriender. Gradually they come to realize that their panic is not going to overwhelm them. They realize that they can enjoy the company of others without feeling destroyed. Little by little they are encouraged to go out by themselves until they attain the confidence to negotiate peer groups without fear or anxiety.

The physical dimension tends to haunt young people who are not sure of themselves with special application to their appearance. Any physical defect is exaggerated but most of the time no physical defect exists. The face is misinterpreted as ugly and the body as misshapen. The intensity with which these convictions are held is astonishing and it approaches a delusional level. Young men insist that their noses, ears, mouths are all wrong and that they look ugly. Women insist that their faces, mouths, lips, breasts are hideous and that they are too fat or too thin. With these intense beliefs goes an extensive trade in plastic surgery. This is not to say that plastic surgery has no place in combating such beliefs. It certainly has. But before it is proceeded with, care needs to be taken to ensure that the personality is strong enough to gain by the change. There are men and women who cannot profit from surgery because their images are so distorted that even if one part is corrected another will be found to be wrong. When surgery is not applicable, young people need their confidence boosted to the point where they can overcome their fear of being unacceptable. This end is achieved by persistent positive acceptance of the individuals accompanying them to social events and showing them that others find them acceptable. Young people with worries about their physical appearance are often anxious about their whole selves, and it is the acceptance of the whole of themselves that achieves the breakthrough in their self-esteem.

Eventually wounded adolescents feel worthless. They are convinced that they are no good and that no one wants them. They reject themselves and find it extremely difficult to accept good feelings. In fact unconsciously they choose friends who are critical of them and in a strange way enjoy being put down and humiliated. This negativity makes them inwardly very unhappy; what on the surface appears to be a flirtation with rejection is underneath a deep wound which approaches despair. These young people need a lot of correct understanding. Superficially they appear reckless, irresponsible, mischievous, hostile and they attract a lot of criticism, and yet they desperately want acceptance and approval.

Healing of such people requires accurate understanding of their basic unhappiness and self-rejection. They need to be approached with an attitude which goes beyond the surface phenomena. When they begin to be accepted unconditionally, they can drop their irritating habits, which are frequently attention-seeking ploys. They need to be reached at the level of their deep unhappiness where they really feel

75

that no one wants them. This sense of rejection can be due to persistent rejection on the part of their families; or they may feel that brothers or sisters have received the lion's share of attention from the parents. They may have grown up in households where their efforts have never been appreciated. Whatever they have achieved has never been thought good enough. Their parents may have spilt up and they are intensely anxious about their security. In all these situations they need some other adult who can give them the feeling that they matter for their own selves; not for their looks, achievements or talents but simply for their own presence and existence. A befriender can give them the feeling of really accepting them on their own merits. Sometimes even this acceptance can present difficulties. These adolescents are really very hungry for attention: but the very intensity of their need makes them feel greedy or selfish. The very attention they want feels forbidden. This is where the befriender or those in charge can help. They can make themselves available to the full and help the adolescents to experience as much attention and care as they need. Slowly such needy individuals may realize that their desires for attention are not wicked and they can have what they want. Their sense of significance rises and they begin to feel they matter as persons in their own right. Suddenly all the resentment of deprivation is unleashed and the person who is befriending is the recipient of much hostility, not anger which is associated with his or her own behaviour but the transferred frustration and annoyance which is linked with a parental figure. The befriender must realize that the angry feelings are a projection of past experiences and has to ride the storm and stay the course until the young person emerges from the interaction and realizes that he is angry unnecessarily now. As trust begins to develop with the counsellor or befriender, there will be periods when the gains are temporarily lost. There will be days when the adolescent regresses to a previous state of mistrust, doubt and uncertainty, testing the befriender repeatedly by questioning his reason for helping. The young person will say, 'You don't care . . . You have to do this caring . . . It isn't real . . . You can't mean what you say . . . I am nothing to you . . . You say the same thing to dozens of people.' The befriender has

76

to stand his ground and really care despite the resistance put up to change. Ultimately change does come and the insecure young person begins to feel safer, accepted and more loveable. He is now ready to risk forming new relationships and will gradually accept care, love and attention from others.

The doubts about self-worth extend to the intellect. Insecure young people also doubt whether they have any intelligence or competence. They think of and treat themselves as stupid. If they are artistic, they will destroy their creative work as being no good. This sense of self-degradation extends to their total intellectual capacities. If they do achieve any success, it is a fluke or accident. They don't believe they can repeat it. Basically they do not link any of their competence with themselves. They feel empty of skill or intelligence and they wonder how they have got so far in life.

The healing response is the same for the intellectual doubts as for the emotional ones. Such young people are encouraged to continue with their studies or other efforts. The fundamental principle of healing is that they matter whatever their achievements. The person befriending needs to extend unconditional acceptance to the adolescent, who feels received with all his limitations and begins to learn that his worth lies in his personhood. The person who feels accepted also discovers within himself his worth as a competent, intelligent person.

Finally, wounded adolescents despair of being loved by anyone, least of all by God. Their sense of despair makes them feel abandoned by everyone. Here the spiritual adviser may fail: the direct response to God's invitation may be a flat refusal even to consider it. The spiritual adviser needs to make it possible for the adolescent to feel accepted by him on a human plane which becomes symbolic of divine acceptance. Instead of despair there may be rebellion. The young person may feel that he cannot subscribe to the tenets he has believed hitherto. Part of this rebellion may be an expression of the autonomy of the individual. In asserting his independence he may feel he wants to question all his beliefs including his faith. The rejection of faith may be very painful to the parents or those who are taking care of the child. But true faith has to be questioned and, if it is going to be accepted authentically, it has to go through this test of fire.

Sometimes the young person goes through a powerful conversion at this stage of his/her life. The sense of aloneness in the human condition is filled by the presence of God, who is a source of comfort and fulfilment. As already mentioned, young people are very sensitive to the needs of others, particularly the poor and the handicapped. A sense of conversion links with this altruism and a sense of caring and loving emerges from this combination.

Most young people leave school at about the age of sixteen and start work. A small number leave school later after further study. Whatever happens the young person starts a new style of living. At school the student had reached the peak of his abilities and felt that he had attained a position of some standing in the academic world. At work he starts at the bottom again. This may be a blow to morale but most youngsters accept the change-over.

There are, however, a small number of youngsters who find it very hard to settle down to work. They appear on the surface lazy but in fact this 'laziness' covers up an extreme reticence and fear of making a mistake and being criticized. Laziness is in fact an unwillingness to subject themselves to the risk of being found incompetent. Once again these young people are living with an inner dread of failure. They are not always aware of this fear. They may in fact sit with a nonchalant air and give a very sophisticated explanation as to why they don't go to work. They may blame the capitalist society, international business, exploitation by employers or even the threat of atomic war. These and similar excuses are held on to with intense feeling because they offer an explanation for an unbearable inner unrest.

Helping such young people is not easy. They are most unwilling to be dragged away from their explanations. In order to achieve any shift, their confidence has to be gained. They have to feel very secure before they will admit their fears of incompetence or failure. This rapport can only be achieved in an atmosphere of trust that their anxieties will be taken seriously and that they will not be ridiculed. For a while they can be given sheltered work, rehabilitation or even a training. But whilst they are learning new work their confidence has to be built up in terms of their personal significance and acceptance.

Another type of work difficulty besets the young person who goes to work but does not stay very long in any job. Such people find mixing with others extremely anxiety-provoking. They get so anxious that they believe others are talking about them. Alternatively they are so sensitive that any remark made by the boss is interpreted as a criticism and received as an insult which is considered intolerable. Thus these young men and women have innumerable jobs moving at regular intervals—easy when there are plenty of jobs but extremely difficult in a depression.

Such young people may come back to their parents or former caretakers and seek help. Their sensitivity and anxiety have to be identified and helped. They need to see how concerned they are about other people's opinion of them and understand their readiness to feel attacked. Their confidence and self-esteem has to be built up so that they can be criticized without feeling destroyed. Indeed, this tendency to take offence at the slightest criticism can be recognized even whilst such adolescents are still under care. Help can be introduced early on and such people made to realize that criticism does not mean rejection. They have to be encouraged to feel that, if one part of them is corrected, it does not mean that the whole of them is wrong. Frequently such people are notoriously aware of criticism and hardly register any praise. They need to be helped to appreciate good experiences and to accept appreciation when it comes their way. Thus their lives will become a more balanced experience of acceptance and criticism. For some, however, the wound of rejection is very deep and such people may need specialized psychological help.

Finally there is the development of attraction, acquaintance and friendship with the opposite sex, gradually during the second decade, particularly in the second half. Boys and girls mix, go out to parties, socials, discos, theatres, outings. They come together in groups and also form individual friendships. Normally there is no problem. But even here self-doubt and lack of self-esteem may rear their ugly heads. I have mentioned the distinct fear of being unattractive. Boys and girls will each find their own specific anxieties about their appearance and some will tend to isolate themselves. Or they will go to dances and stand on the fringe of things because they don't expect that anyone will want to associate with them. These young people need to have their confidence built up repeatedly until such time as they can begin to rely on their intrinsic value and worth.

The ability to separate from parents, find a job and mix and relate with the opposite sex are essential stages of the development of the adolescent. When young people achieve these objectives they have clarified their identity and are moving in the direction of being adults. Adolescence is a stage when the person is no longer a child and yet has not quite reached the status of being an adult. If this phase of transition is not completed, then the young person is said to have the problem of identity confusion. Such confusion exists when, instead of independence, dependence is persisted with; when instead of work, inactivity is persisted with; when, instead of moving forward towards a person of the other sex, isolation is maintained.

In the presence of identity confusion or adolescent crisis, the adolescent is the last person to realize what is wrong. The surrounding adults on the other hand have a marvellous opportunity to give a helping hand to overcome these difficulties. It usually takes some time to negotiate these various anxieties, but patience over months and sometimes years is rewarded with the success of moving a young girl or boy through the threshold of adolescence to the opening door of adulthood.

13

Marriage

This book has been devoted to the growth of love and sexuality in the first two decades of life; since marriage usually occurs in the middle of the third decade, it would appear to be out of place. This is not really the case, for one of the objectives of modern education is to prepare young people for human relationships of which marriage is the most fundamental. If we have some knowledge of what is expected in contemporary marriage, then young people can be given some idea of what to anticipate.

Concept of contemporary marriage
What sort of marriage can young people look forward to? Traditionally marriage has been an institution with fixed roles. Since the industrial revolution—when home and work were separated—there have been traditional roles for the sexes in marriage. Men have gone out of the home to work, had the responsibility of looking after the family economically and of acting as the leader of the family, taking charge of important decisions. The wife has been responsible for looking after the home, having children and nurturing them and being the catalyst of tenderness and affection. These roles still exist but there have been significant changes in marriage. The main change has been the emancipation of women. In terms of education, status and economic standing, women have achieved a great deal, and this means that the relationship between the sexes is changing. The change is most clearly seen in marriage. Here the roles of the sexes have become much more fluid. Women also go out to work, thus gaining a certain degree of economic independence. Men are helping more in household activities and looking after the children a good deal more. Women's standing has

been raised and the result is that communication has been increased and decisions are taken after mutual discussion. This does not mean that the traditional roles have disappeared, but it does mean that there is much greater equity between the sexes.

Another factor which is also contributing to change in marriage in the West is the material transformation. As living standards improve and there is greater security in food, shelter and work, men and women imperceptibly broaden their awareness of their needs. As material requirements are met, there is a deepening quest and another layer of the personality is engaged: the world of feeling, emotions and sexuality.

As a result of all these changes, contemporary marriage in the West takes different shapes. Couples meet and become involved with each other as a sociological phenomenon of moving on to another stage in life and at the same time on a more romantic basis. Love and affection play a greater part than in the past although not so great as is usually thought. There is an appropriate time for marriage, which is negotiated on a much more affective basis than in the past, though it is still the need to get married which is uppermost. Having got married, the couple relate much more on a basis of intimacy. Feelings and emotions play a much greater role than in the past. In the past the important issue was the execution of roles. Provided spouses were good at their respective roles of looking after the family and the home then the marriage was considered to be good. These roles remain important but now, as already mentioned, expectations have changed to include fulfilment at the level of feelings, emotions and sexuality. The couple are much closer to each other and their inner psychological worlds engage in new expectations of fulfilment. What are these expectations? They are basically three and consist of sustaining, healing and growth. So far sustaining has been carried out by the parent or caretaker, now it is mutual. Healing is a feature which has been present throughout the previous two decades and continues in marriage, and finally there is an extension of growth.

Sustaining

At the beginning of marriage both women and men work. The evidence is, however, that women make any sacrifice needed so that their husband's career remains intact. They put his work first and their own second. Thus they are prepared to go where the husband's job is, to change their work pattern to fit in with his, and generally they arrange their work to fit in with his career. This means that, although women have attained some economic independence, they are still dependent on their husbands for ultimate economic support.

After an initial interval of perhaps a year or two there will be mutual agreement to start a family, and with this step the wife withdraws from work whilst her children are young. During this period the husband assumes sole responsibility for the economic sustenance of the home and the family reverts to the traditional roles. The average family size is about two children; when they have been born and reach school age many women return to work and once again there are two incomes. Except where the woman's job is highly paid, the woman's income is usually small compared to that of her husband and, contrary to the view that it supplies the luxuries of the home, the wife's income often simply sustains the economic viability of the household. Thus, whilst women certainly play a much greater role in the economic sustaining of the home and some mutual contribution is achieved, the husband still remains the main contributor.

It is in another area, however, that a new system of support has emerged. In the intimacy of the new relationship, feelings play a much greater role and the couple expect emotional sustaining from each other; that is to say that they expect from each other a sensitive response to the worries, mood changes and anxieties of their inner world. In traditional marriage such a communication may have taken place but it was not an *expected* response from the spouse. Now it is. Each spouse is expected to communicate, feel sensitively and respond accurately to the other's feelings. In this change women have a distinct advantage, since they can handle feelings much more easily. Men do not find it easy to cope with emotions, and one of the useful preparations for marriage is to get boys more attuned to feelings.

What is certainly clear is that when marriages get into difficulties one of the main complaints is the inability of the husband to cope with the wife's feelings. Husbands often complain that the world of women is a mystery to them; by that they mean that they do not understand or appreciate the world of feelings.

Healing

If the interaction of sustaining is accomplished satisfactorily, then there emerges an intimacy between the couple which allows the wounds that are brought by both partners to be revealed. Healing has been emphasized in this book in each decade. Marriage lasts for several decades, and the ultimate healing takes place in this relationship.

The wounds that are brought into marriage come from two sources. The first is genetic inheritance. It is well known that the tendency to depression, anxiety, anger is up to a point inherited. The second source of wounds has been frequently referred to and arises from the failure of nurturing. Thus men and women grow up with deficits in feelings of trust, self-esteem, confidence, security, loveability and worthiness. Couples come to marriage with these wounds and once again expect their partner to understand and respond positively to them. Thus, if one partner lacks confidence, the other is expected to be encouraging and reassuring. If one feels unloveable, the other is expected to offer unconditional loving which makes a profound difference. Various fears such as agoraphobia or claustrophobia can be modified by encouragement and support. Feelings of rejection and unacceptance can also be altered as the partners make each other feel really wanted.

As with sustaining, healing needs a sensitive awareness of the needs of the partner. The partner gives the spouse a second opportunity to experience what was missed in childhood or to correct the distortions of the nurturing experience. Failure of healing is one of the main complaints in marital breakdown. Women often complain that their husbands do not appreciate their need for freedom, initiative, acceptance, tenderness and recognition; instead these husbands continue the childhood responses of being critical, rejecting, negative, jealous, envious and selfish.

If, on the other hand, healing does occur, then something uniquely important takes place. In fact healing does occur in a number of marriages and from the Christian point of view this is something marvellous. It means in fact that marriage becomes the central place of healing in society and it is the place where divine and human love meet and interact.

In order to help this healing, young people have to be sensitized to each other's needs, problems and difficulties. They have to realize that they are capable of being therapists to other people by being available in a way which reproduces the original distorted experience and provides the other with another opportunity to experience what was missing in love or understanding. This capacity to be a therapist to another person by being available and offering what was missing in the first intimate relationship between parent and child is a basic concept of human interaction which involves all of us and should be part of our educational training.

Growth

If a person's wounds are marked and unyielding, most of his energy is taken up emotionally with mere survival. The really hurt person struggles from one day to another to overcome the feeling of being unwanted or unloveable. Such people do not have much time or energy for anything else. If, however, their wounds ameliorate, they have the opportunity to grow and mature.

Growth takes place socially, physically, intellectually, emotionally and spiritually. At the social level men and women learn to appreciate the social signals which are necessary to interact with each other. They check and test authenticity and learn to distinguish between real friends and those who hold on parasitically to get what they can from the relationship.

Social growth is the advance in social skills so that isolation is overcome and group formation with others outside the home occurs. In Christian marriage social activity opens the whole family to the world outside, and in this way others are befriended who need the shelter and support of family life. The outsider can be the poor, the widow, the fringe person such as the homosexual, those in difficulties, the separated and/or divorced, in fact all those who need special loving because of their personal circumstances.

Physical growth is difficult to grasp. By the time we get married we have reached the limits of our growth, at least in height. Later on our girth will expand, but that is not considered an advantage! Real physical growth is the transformation of the body into an athletic entity with all the sacrifices that both partners have to make to allow time for training. Alternative training can be received for artistic work. In both instances the body is transformed from a mass of untrained and unco-ordinated musculature into a highly efficient and effective organism.

Intellectual growth is also a challenging idea. Our maximum I.Q. is also reached by the time we get married. There are late developers, but they are the exceptions. Most people have their intellectual make-up settled by the time they leave school. But, independently of what the absolute intelligence of the person is, what happens over the years is the gradual transformation of intellect into wisdom. Ideas are checked and tested and, depending on the results, there grows a sense of what is appropriate and of value. This sense of wisdom, often called experience, is highly valued and makes a great difference in our ordinary dealings. Some of this wisdom is acquired at work and with friends but a great deal is developed at home.

Emotional growth is related ultimately to the capacity to love. Loving is concerned with the love of self and our neighbour and God. Love of self is a concept that raises eyebrows. It is associated with selfishness and egoism; and yet it is nothing of the sort. It is simply a question of the maximum possession of ourselves. The more we possess ourselves, the more of ourselves we have to offer to others in and through availability. This love of self is the basic background to the love of others and of God. How do we love others? At the heart of emotional growth is the capacity to be empathetically aware of the needs of our neighbours. These needs can be material, but, as stressed throughout the book, it is their inner world of feelings that urgently need to be felt and responded to accurately. Perhaps the single most important act of loving is to affirm our neighbours. Usually we do the opposite of affirmation. We think that we love our spouses best by pointing out what's wrong with them! We feel that if we correct them all the time, they will ultimately learn correct behaviour. There is no doubt that we must point out what is wrong but—even more important— we need to praise and appreciate the good things that our partners do. Indeed, we have to affirm not only our spouses but our children as well. Affirmation is the ultimate act of loving in our everyday experiences. Of course there is sacrificial loving which in the end demands that one person gives his life for another. We are not ordinarily called to give up our lives for our neighbours, but we are constantly needed to affirm and confirm their goodness.

Ultimately our love has to be directed to God. God is an unseen and unknown mystery. We move in our love of God from neighbour to the Almighty. In loving our neighbours we do in fact love God, but ultimately we have to relate to the mystery of the personhood of God. In this personhood Jesus Christ stands out as the best defined person of the Trinity. The incarnation made him real in a sense the other two members of the Trinity are not. But through Jesus Christ we find our way to God the Father and Holy Spirit.

Permanency
We can now see that if we are to sustain, heal and grow we need continuous, reliable and predictable relations: in other words we need permanency in marriage. It is often said that Christianity has invented permanency of marriage as a form of imprisonment. It is an invention of Christianity to keep men and women glued to each other against their will. In fact the opposite is the case. The very nature of loving requires permanency and in recommending permanency as the ideal, all that Christianity is doing is safeguarding that which is most human.

It is the most human environment for the sustaining, healing and growth of the partners but also for the needs of their children, who certainly need continuity, reliability and predictability in order to thrive.

Sexuality
So far the loving or affective side of marriage has been mentioned, for ultimately marriages survive on the presence

or absence of love. But throughout this book what has been proposed as being most fully human is the conjunction of love and sex.

Sexual intercourse is most fully expressed in this conjunction. The couple who share the affection mentioned are also attracted physically and want to give expression to this desire. Intercourse takes place. Traditionally such intercourse was seen as having primarily a procreative potential and a loving capacity. The loving capacity is clearly seen in the union that sex brings about. Sexual intercourse however has not only a general but also a specific loving meaning. It has its own body language. This language has several expressions.

When the couple make love, naturally they rejoice in the pleasure they experience. Thus coitus assumes an expression of thanksgiving for making the pleasure possible. Thanksgiving is a profound experience of gratitude for what the couple have shared with each other. If the act has been pleasurable, the couple wish to repeat it. Thus another point of coitus is the recurrent hope that it raises that the couple will stay together to enjoy further sexual activity. Beyond gratitude and hope there is reconciliation. Almost all married people know that, after a row or quarrel which is resolved, coitus can seal the reconciliation or sometimes even initiate it. Gratitude, hope and reconciliation are followed by the affirmation of sexual identity. There is no more powerful way of recurrently affirming the fact that one is a woman and desired as such or a man and equally desired as such than through intercourse. And in the most comprehensive reassurance of all, the husband and wife assert repeatedly through intercourse that they recognize, want, appreciate and love each other as complete persons. If healing is needed in any of these areas, then sexual intercourse provides through its bodily language a most powerful means of consolidating the relationship.

Children
In the whole of the Christian tradition, sex and procreation have been intimately related, and indeed for a long period intercourse was only justified if procreation was specifically intended. This view is no longer held, and the widespread

88

advent of birth control is a sign of the separation of intercourse from procreation. The Roman Catholic Church, which, as do all the other Churches, permits and encourages birth regulation, nevertheless insists that sexual acts should remain open to new life and so prohibits all methods other than natural means of birth regulation.

But all Christians still recognize that having children is a precious gift from God. In procreation parents become co-authors of life and in doing so assume all the love and creativity that inspires God to create and love humanity. Having and raising children remains a unique privilege for parents, who are not only maintaining the world but are raising life which is destined for a relationship of love with God.

The size of the modern family is small and the possible range of sexual activity immense as it covers some fifty years of marriage. Thus ninety-nine per cent of sexual activity is knowingly non-procreative. During this majority of sexual acts it is the intrinsic features of sexual intercourse that matter. So every effort should be made to make coitus as rich an act as possible so that its loving characteristics are fully realized.

Marital Breakdown
Whilst the vast majority of marriages survive, the divorce rate remains high and involves currently one in four marriages and in some instances one in three. These instances involve young people and a few words about these risks are appropriate in this chapter.

A good deal of research has shown that youthful marriages are particularly vulnerable to marriage breakdown. Brides under the age of twenty are taking major risks, and marriages where both brides and bridegrooms are under the age of twenty are particularly susceptible to divorce. The reason is that some of these marriages are escapes from painful home situations and the only force that welds the relationship is the desire to escape from that situation. Hasty marriages in this young age are also risky propositions. The young people concerned have not had the time to get to know each other, and a minimum knowledge is essential if the marriage is to survive.

Another factor associated with marital breakdown is premarital pregnancy. In the past premarital pregnancy was an absolute indication for a hasty marriage. We now know that, if the couple do not love one another, then a fixed marriage is the last thing that should occur. The alternatives are a termination of pregnancy or the continuation of the pregnancy with or without adoption in mind. Termination of pregnancy is not consistent with the Christian conscience and neither is a hurried marriage; consequently continuation of the pregnancy with adequate support for the girl is the only tenable alternative.

Marital breakdown is also associated with low socio-economic groups. This does not mean that the poor are doomed to divorce. What it means is that it is in this group that couples marry early, have more premarital pregnancies, poor housing and economic conditions and are therefore generally disadvantaged.

If young couples are to marry, then there are a few more warning signals which they ought to heed. If their courtship has been a stormy one with a number of separations and reconciliations, then it is important for them to realize that such courtships also herald stormy marriages. This means that if the man is prone to heavy drinking, gambling or aggressive behaviour, then it is important that these patterns of behaviour should change before the couple get married: they should not hope for a conversion afterwards. The other point to remember, particularly in the low socio-economic group, is that parents remain a source of strong support for the young couple. Any permanent opposition between parents and their children to the forthcoming marriage should be avoided. In particular the relationship between daughter and mother is important and forms a very important sustaining influence in the marriage.

Those who have young people under their care should be familiar with these adverse characteristics, and preparation for marriage should carry these warnings.

Support for marriage
Perhaps one of the most obvious weaknesses in the Christian tradition is the fact that marriage has been seen as a great event beginning and ending on the wedding day. After the

wedding the couple are forgotten until their first baby is born and the family is brought into contact with the Church through baptism, first communion and confirmation. The couple seem to be lost and there is no pastoral service to the married couple as such.

It seems to me important that the married need a service to themselves irrespective of the presence of children. The couple need to be supported in their own task of initiating and maintaining their marriage, and in this respect parents, caretakers and others have an important role in keeping close to the young people and supporting, without interfering, in the early years of marriage.

Two relationships
It will be clear by now that there are two intimate relationships in life. The first is between ourselves and our parents and the second is between ourselves and our spouses. The quality of the second relationship is intimately related to that of the first. It is in the first relationship that we learn how to be loved and in the second one that we offer this love to our most precious neighbours, our partners in marriage.